MESA MEXICANA

MESA MEXICANA

MARY SUE MILLIKEN AND SUSAN FENIGER
with Helene Siegel

William Morrow and Company, Inc.
New York

ALSO BY MARY SUE MILLIKEN AND SUSAN FENIGER
WITH HELENE SIEGEL

CITY CUISINE

It is the policy of William Morrow and company, Inc., and its imprints and affiliates, recoognizing the importance of preserving what has been written, to print the books we publish on acid-free paper, and we exert our best efforts to that end.

Library of Congress Cataloging-in-Publication Data

Milliken, Mary Sue.
Mesa Mexicana / Mary Sue Milliken and Susan Feniger with
Helene Siegel.
p.   cm.
Includes index.
ISBN 0-688-10649-8
1. Cookery, Mexican.   2. Border Grill (Restaurant)   I. Feniger,
Susan.   II. Siegel, Helene.   III. Title.
TX716.M4M55   1994
641.5972—dc20   93-43099
                                                                                    CIP

Printed in the United States of America

2 3 4 5 6 7 8 9 10

THIS IS DEDICATED TO THE ONES WE LOVE

DANAE AND JOSH

ACKNOWLEDGMENTS

Our thanks to the always-inventive kitchen staff of Border Grill and especially to

Tacho Kneeland	Ruth Milliken	Barbara Leopold
Toni Sakaguchi	Kim Muller	Jean Pierre Rodriguez
Linda Bergh	Karen Norby	Christian Schirmer

whose generous help and patient perfectionism helped develop many of the recipes contained in these pages.

Our thanks to Eulalia Salsas and the Kneeland family in Mexico City, whose introduction to the Mexican kitchen was an unforgettable and inspirational experience.

Our thanks to Su Huntley and Donna Muir, whose paintings bring life to Border Grill walls and ceilings, menus, coasters, napkins, matches, toothpicks . . . and now this cookbook.

Our thanks to Helene Siegel, who captures our passionate ramblings about food and cooking in succinct, clear text that is delightful to read and easy to understand.

Our thanks to Mike Fink, our enduring ally for superb graphics, who visually distills the essence of what we do.

Our thanks to Phil Capice, whose support and confidence made it possible for the Border Grill to persevere, and, consequently, this book to be written.

And special thanks to Ann Bramson, our editor, as always the epitome of patience.

Contents

Introduction

One of the things that attracted us to Latin food from the start, perhaps as a reaction to our strict French training as chefs, was its easy informality and the generosity of those who cook and serve it naturally. As for the flavors, they were simple, direct, and strong—all qualities we craved after the subtleties of French cuisine.

Like most Americans, our first exposure to Mexican food was the heavily sauced combination plates of our youth. As soon as we started working in restaurant kitchens, however, and tasted the real thing, we were blown away. Our fellow workers, who were mostly Latino, shared light, quick salsas and chile-laced stews for lunch that sent us combing Los Angeles's barrios for authentic taco stands and small family restaurants. Eventually our curiosity led us to Mexico—just four hundred miles south of Los Angeles, but many more miles away culinarily.

Our first trip took us to Mexico City, where, under the wing of a fabulous home cook named Eulalia Salsas, we got an overview of the various regional styles. She took us to the markets daily and invited us into her kitchen to watch her cook. It soon became apparent that real Mexican cooking called for a sophisticated variety of ingredients and techniques unknown to us in Los Angeles.

On subsequent trips south, we explored the incredibly fresh fish cocktails and ceviches of Veracruz along the Gulf Coast, the exotic southern foods of Oaxaca and neighboring Guatemala, and the stews of central Puebla, but the region we keep going back to is the eastern peninsula of the Yucatán. We love the play of orange-tinged achiote against a sweet banana leaf, turkey in sweet-and-sour escabeche topped with pungent red onions and the deep yellow corn masa we first discovered there. In Mérida, the capital city, there is a Portuguese and Spanish influence on native foods that we find mesmerizing.

As chefs and serious sensory junkies, we have found an exciting new vocabulary to work with from the world of Mexican food. With some ingredients like smoky dried chipotle chiles it was love at first sight, and with others like the herb epazote it took some time for affection and understanding to grow. Now our world is a richer place for having their unique tastes in it.

We encourage our readers to keep an open mind and palate when it comes to trying new ethnic foods or methods of cooking. As our mothers once asked, "How do you know you don't like it if you won't even taste it?" Or, on a more planetary note, eating a wider variety of foods keeps more foods growing for a wider variety of people.

On the subject of ingredients, we recommend shopping at local farmers' markets and organic markets whenever possible. Fruits and vegetables raised by small producers may not look quite as pretty as those sold at the supermarket but experience has taught us that ugly often means better when it comes to fruits and vegetables. And if you are concerned with eating healthfully, you will find a wealth of recipes here that provide a good balance of grains and vegetables to meat. Just reserve that gaucho steak or spicy baby back ribs for special occasions and eat from the bottom of the pyramid regularly, as we do.

As we mentioned before, one of the strong attractions of the Mexican kitchen for us was its people. We have always respected the Latinos we have worked alongside in the restaurant kitchen. To us, they are the swiftest butchers and the best natural cooks and we love the spirit of fun they bring to kitchen work.

It is not really surprising that Mexican food is often perceived as party food. It is inexpensive food that belongs heaped on platters and shared family style. If, at times, the kitchen work seems daunting, then invite friends and family to help stuff tamales or pat out tortillas and start the party early. After all, the fun begins in the kitchen!

Pointers on Ingredients and Techniques

Ingredients

Kosher Salt and Freshly Ground Black Pepper

We like to begin our cooking classes by advising students to throw out their salt shakers and pre-ground or cracked pepper and rethink the way they use these two sturdy ingredients. That usually wakes them up.

To us, these are great flavor enhancers that are too often overlooked, added at the last moment or, even worse (for those without health problems), totally eliminated. We couldn't live without them.

Salt is probably the most important ingredient in this book. We recommend keeping a small dish of kosher or coarse salt near your range at home and adding it with your fingertips as you cook. You can control the amount much better that way than by shaking.

When cooking with salt, it is important to add it in stages. We like to evenly salt all meat, fish and poultry on both sides before cooking. For stews and soups we add salt at the sauté stage (usually with onions and garlic) to spread its flavor. If you add salt only at the end, it just sits on top and screams "salt." Adding salt at the end should be just a final adjustment.

If you are trying to use less or eliminate salt, try intensifying your other spices, herbs and acid flavors to make up for the loss.

Freshly ground black pepper balances other strong flavors with its own bright, aromatic perfume. The pre-cracked or ground product sold in the market lost its perfume long ago, when it was first processed. We recommend keeping a good pepper mill (Peugeot is great) at your side in the kitchen as you cook.

SPANISH OLIVE OIL

Spanish olive oil, especially the G. Sensat brand, is one of our recent discoveries. Spanish or Greek olive oil has a fruitier, slightly stronger flavor than Italian olive oil and it is a much better value. We love it in all our cooking.

HERBS AND SEASONINGS

CILANTRO, or fresh coriander or Chinese parsley, is a thin-leafed bright green herb, similar in appearance to Italian parsley, that has a taste and aroma all its own. It is usually either passionately loved or hated. We fall into the lovers' camp. It is key to the Mexican kitchen and easily found in the supermarket.

EPAZOTE is a wild green herb considered de rigueur in Mexico for cooking black beans and certain quesadillas. It will grow easily, like the weed that it is, in the garden. Even for us, its pungent aroma was an acquired taste, although now Susan particularly adores it. Epazote adds complexity that is incomparable. We cannot imagine a substitute.

OREGANO is the most common cooking herb in Mexico, where thirteen varieties are grown. Although we sometimes use the fresh herb, when we use it dried, we often toast it first in a dry pan.

ACHIOTE PASTE is a bright orange seasoning paste from the Yucatán made of ground annatto seeds, oregano, cumin, cinnamon, pepper and cloves. It often is thinned with vinegar or citrus juices for marinades and sauces and should always be cooked first to remove any chalkiness. This is what produces the bright orange color often found in Mexican food, so be sure to wash off any utensils that touch it or they just might remain orange. The paste is sold in bricks in Mexican markets and can be kept well wrapped in the refrigerator for a long time.

FRUITS AND VEGETABLES

CHILE PEPPERS A great deal of mystique has come to surround chile peppers, but don't be daunted by the hype. They are no more difficult to work with than any vegetable and they deliver a great deal of pizzazz for very little cost. You probably will come to love them, or at least respect them, as we do, once you just jump in and start cooking with and tasting them. Here are some minimal guidelines.

In general, do not shop by name when looking for chiles, as they go by different names in different regions of the country. It is wiser to shop by appearance, since chances are a chile that looks like the one described will taste similar. On the other hand, appearance is not necessarily an indication of heat. You can only learn by trying and tasting. Here are the chiles we rely on most:

chiles

ANCHO is the dried brown wide-shouldered poblano pepper that delivers the mellowest sweet bell pepper flavor. The ancho chile is often julienned and added to sauces for its texture as well as its rich, peppery flavor. It is also pureed to add body at the beginning of a sauce. Look for anchos with pliable rather than brittle skin and store, wrapped in plastic, in the freezer. Be careful when toasting anchos as they can easily burn and grow bitter. Just pass them over a burner or grill quickly (a few seconds each side is fine), *not* to blacken. Mulatos or negros are good substitutes.

CHIPOTLES, the dried and smoked version of ripened jalapeños, are probably our favorite chile. Susan can still remember her first taste of

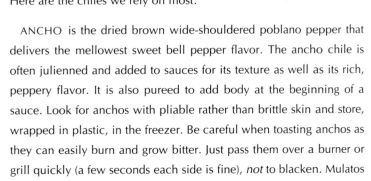

chipotle on our trip to Mexico in 1984. It tasted like bacon in a chile—something she wanted to smell all day. This hot, smoky little chile adds such an intricate dimension to anything it touches that we tend to think of it more as a vegetable than a secondary spice. If they are difficult to find dried, substitute canned chipotles in adobo sauce (and wipe them off if necessary) or small moritas, which are less smoky but spicier. (Use fewer moritas than chipotles.)

ÁRBOLS are the easiest chiles to find. They are the thin, papery, dried red chiles often sold in the supermarket as Chinese hot peppers. They are mouth-searingly hot, and we like to combine their heat with acid or richness for balance.

HABANEROS are pure heat. They are a small, orange lantern-shaped chile that should be handled with respect, if not downright suspicion. We always remove the seeds, and we prefer the taste of fresh to dried.

JALAPEÑOS AND SERRANOS are the workhorses of the Mexican kitchen. The small green peppers are less hot but more peppery than ár-bols and habaneros, and the red ones have an even sweeter, more pep-pery flavor. These are the great garnishing chiles and can be used more or less interchangeably, though the serrano is hotter than the jalapeño.

SERRANOS

POBLANOS are our favorite fresh green chile. They are a medium-sized thick-skinned wide-shouldered sometimes spicy chile excellent for stuffing for chiles rellenos and roasting for soups, salads, sauces and rajas (roasted pepper strips). In some parts of the country they are mis-labeled pasillas, which are lighter green and skinnier. When shopping, look for bigger ones, which are better for stuffing and roasting. Hotness can vary greatly in this particular chile. Anaheims, though less spicy, can be substituted.

AVOCADO We prefer Haas, the pebbly-skinned medium-sized av-ocado from California and Mexico, in all our cooking. It has a richer, nuttier flavor that is far superior to other varieties.

TOMATILLOS are small, round green fruits in papery husks sometimes mistakenly called green tomatoes. They have a much sharper, acidic taste than tomatoes and we adore them both raw and cooked. Look for tomatillos with tightly wrapped husks for the freshest flavor.

LIMES appear as a seasoning at almost every Mexican meal. They are used as much for their distinctive flavor as for their acidity, which stands out where lemon's flavor often blends in. When shopping for limes, look for larger, yellowish ones that are not so pretty. They generally have more juice and better flavor. If only small impossibly hard limes are available, substitute lemons.

TAMARIND is a dried brown seed pod that produces a deliciously sticky sweet-sour paste when cooked. One of the key ingredients in Worcestershire sauce, it is popular in Indian, Mexican and Thai cuisines. It is sold in bulk paste as well as pod form in ethnic markets.

PLANTAINS are the thick-skinned, starchy bananas used for cooking in Latin countries. Look for thoroughly blackened skins, which indicate they are ripe; you can hasten ripening of greener plantains by storing under newspapers.

Dairy

MEXICAN CREMA, similar to crème fraîche, is used frequently as a garnish, dressing or spread. Although it is sweeter than sour cream, sour cream is a good substitute. Crema, or crème fraîche, is sold in the refrigerator case at some supermarkets, or you can make your own (see page 249).

CHEESE is quite popular in the Mexican kitchen, thanks to the influence of the Spanish. We like to use a grated mixture of one part *manchego,* one part *panela* and one-half part *Cotija* because it gives greater texture and flavor than just one cheese, but that is not a hard-and-fast rule. Go right ahead and use whatever you happen to have in the house, or experiment and come up with your own cheese mix. Here is some help in identifying Mexican cheeses:

MANCHEGO There are two kinds of *manchego* used in Mexican cooking—and neither is the high-priced Spanish variety sold in upscale cheese shops. There is a hard variety (called *viejo*) and a soft, semifirm, golden one that is an excellent melter. The soft one is used most often for cooking. Monterey Jack or muenster can be substituted.

AÑEJO, also known as *Cotija,* is a salty, crumbly white cheese, similar to feta in appearance. Romano or washed and dried feta are good substitutes.

PANELA is a mild, milky-tasting, fresh white cheese often sold in rounds. A ricotta, farmer's or dry cottage cheese can be substituted.

LARD

Although we are perfectly happy at the restaurant to substitute vegetable shortening on request, we find the current fear of lard irrational. Is it any healthier to eat an eight-ounce sirloin than a great Guatemalan tamale with some lard-whipped masa? To our minds, fat is fat, and whether it comes from chicken, beef or pork, it has its place. We use it in our cooking for its special flavor and eat it moderately. We think the fear of lard may stem from the days when people ate huge quantities of fried foods. But in these leaner times, a little bit of lard now and then can't really do any damage and it sure does add flavor.

MASA

Masa is the Spanish word for dough. Masa harina is flour. Corn masa is made of dried corn cooked with limestone and ground with water. It is ground to different consistencies according to its eventual use (thin dough is for tortillas and thick, rich dough is for tamales). Masa labeled ''preparada para tamales'' will not work in our tamale recipes because it already has fat and seasonings added. We prefer a deep yellow rough-hewn masa harina to whiter varieties because it has a pronounced sweet-corn flavor. We are currently addicted to masa from the Aztec Milling Company here in Los Angeles (213–722–8041). Ask for Maseca regular yellow number 0; if they will ship it to you, prepare to be transported.

TORTILLAS

While homemade corn tortillas are a delight we fully describe on page 132, we all have days when there just isn't enough time for patting out masa. When shopping for tortillas, try to buy them in a market where there is a large demand so they have a better chance of being fresh. Check the date on the package and look for packages sealed airtight. Freshness makes a huge difference in tortillas just as it does in bread. We prefer deep yellow rather than pale corn tortillas and recommend the small size for tacomaking. As for flour tortillas, some markets sell the uncooked dough, usually in the freezer case near the frozen pizza dough. It makes a good fresh, warm tortilla.

GRilled pepper

SOME VALUABLE TECHNIQUES

ROASTING AND TOASTING

Traditional Mexican foods like moles, fideo and tortilla soups and rice depend upon the depth of flavor that results from roasting and toasting. Here are some specifics:

FRESH CHILES and bell peppers can be roasted over a gas flame or on a tray under the broiler. Keep turning so the skin is evenly charred, without burning and drying out the flesh. Transfer charred peppers to a plastic bag, tie the top closed and let steam until cool to the touch, about fifteen minutes. (If you are rushed, you can place the bag in a bowl of iced water to speed things up.) The best way to peel is just to pull off the charred skin by hand and then dip the peppers briefly in water to remove any blackened bits. Do not peel the pepper under running water since that will wash away flavorful juices. Once peeled, cut away stems, seeds and veins.

DRIED CHILES such as anchos are lightly toasted just to soften and develop flavor but never to blacken. Place over a low gas flame or on the grill and heat a few seconds on each side, just until soft.

TOMATOES, TOMATILLOS, ONIONS AND GARLIC are best roasted on a tray under the broiler. Husk the tomatillos and peel the onions and garlic. Arrange the vegetables on a tray, taking care to tuck the garlic under larger vegetables to prevent blackening. Stay nearby and keep turning until everything but the garlic is totally blackened. The garlic should just turn golden. When transferring these roasted ingredients to a container, be sure to add all the juices from the pan and the blackened skin since they add the smoky flavor you are striving for.

SEEDS, such as coriander and cumin, develop a fuller flavor with roasting. Simply place in a dry pan over medium heat and keep shaking and tossing the pan until their aroma is released, no more than a minute.

WORKING WITH CHILES

Although we do specify chile quantities in these recipes, those figures are open to interpretation. Once you gain some experience, and know who you are cooking for, you can adjust the number of chiles according to taste. Just bear in mind that the seeds and veins are hotter than the flesh. Remove them for less heat or leave them in and chop them to intensify the heat.

MARINATION

Now that mass-produced meats like chicken and pork have lost much of their flavor, we as chefs find ourselves relying on stronger marinades to put some oomph back into the product. An especially flavorful marinade can even take the place of a sauce. As a general rule, marinades should be very strong for the flavors to really make a difference. The less time you have to marinate, the stronger a mixture you need for the flavors to sink in at all. For really short times, we sometimes compensate by brushing the meat with the marinade as it cooks.

COOKING WITH DRIED SPICES

Spices should never just be dropped into a boiling liquid when making a sauce, stew or soup. To really develop their flavors, spices should be cooked first in fat, as you would the onion and garlic at the beginning of a dish, to release their oils and spread their flavors throughout the dish.

FLASH FOOD

Many of the quick, delicious dishes in this book (like the squid sauté on page 183 or the spiced shrimps on page 181) call for flash cooking in a very hot pan—something newer cooks may be reluctant to do. Here is how: Place a dry pan over a high flame and heat the pan without any fat. Meanwhile, be sure your ingredients are seasoned and ready nearby. When the pan is hot, add a high-burning-point fat such as oil (not butter) to the pan. It should immediately smoke. Then add your ingredients—and ignore the instinct to remove the pan from the heat (we have seen even trained chefs do this). It is this very intense heat that quickly seals in juices and produces the fresh, clear flavor desirable in such a dish.

BEAN COOKERY

When cooking any type of dried bean, never add salt to the pot (it will toughen the skins), and always cook with the cover on to prevent drying. To test for doneness, taste a few of the smallest beans. If their centers are smooth and creamy, not powdery, the beans are done.

WASHING THE GREENS

Here is an easy technique for spotlessly cleaning leafy greens such as lettuces and herbs: Fill a sink or large bowl with cold water and add the greens. Let soak a few minutes. Then, carefully lift the leaves out of the water and shake off excess moisture. All the sand and grit will remain at the bottom.

PUREEING GARLIC

To puree garlic in quantity, break the bulbs apart and peel, by first flattening the cloves with the flat side of a heavy knife or cleaver, then removing the skin. Puree with a small amount of olive oil in a food processor fitted with a metal blade or in a blender. Store in the refrigerator for as long as a week.

BLENDER

Beverages

Homemade fruit juices and sangrias are a beautiful, personal way to entertain. Instead of opening a bottle of wine or putting some sodas on ice for your next party, try filling glass punch bowls and pitchers with brilliant tart red Jamaica flower water, fruity deep brown tamarind water or sparkling white wine sangria as we do at the restaurant. They all match terrifically well with Latin flavors and add an extra dash of color and charm to the table.

TAMARIND WATER

Makes 2 ½ quarts

1 ½ pounds dried tamarind pods or 1 pound pulp with seeds

1 gallon water

1 cup sugar

DRIED TAMARIND PODS ARE USUALLY SOLD IN BULK BINS AT LATIN MARKETS, WHERE THE PULP CAN ALSO BE FOUND ALREADY PROCESSED AND PRESSED INTO A BRICK. THE THICK BROWN PULP MAKES AN EXCEPTIONALLY FRUITY SWEET-AND-SOUR JUICE THAT IS PERFECT WITH HOT, SPICY FOODS.

Remove and discard the hard outer pods of the dried tamarind. Combine the remaining dried tamarind or the prepared pulp with the water and bring to a boil. Cook over medium heat about 30 minutes, or until the flesh is very soft, occasionally stirring and mashing with a whisk to break up the flesh and separate the seeds.

Strain and discard the solids. Cool to room temperature and chill. Serve in tall glasses with plenty of ice.

CHIA LIME WATER

Makes 9 cups

2 quarts water

1 cup freshly squeezed lime juice

1 cup sugar

¼ cup chia seeds

several sprigs of fresh sage for garnish (optional)

CHIA ARE TINY GRAY-WHITE SEEDS, SMALLER THAN SESAME, SOLD IN THE SPICE SECTION OF SOME MEXICAN MARKETS AND HEALTH FOOD STORES. IF YOU CANNOT FIND THEM, DON'T LET THAT KEEP YOU FROM MAKING THIS EASY LIMEADE—THEY ARE MOSTLY FOR TEXTURE RATHER THAN TASTE.

Stir together the water, lime juice and sugar until the sugar is dissolved. Stir in the chia seeds and garnish with the optional sage sprigs. Serve in tall glasses over ice.

JAMAICA FLOWER WATER

Makes 1 1/2 quarts

2 quarts water

3/4 cup dried Jamaica or hibiscus flowers

1/2 cup sugar or honey

orange slices for garnish

HIBISCUS FLOWERS MAKE A BRILLIANT TART RED DRINK—HIGH IN VITAMIN C—THAT IS POPULAR ALL OVER MEXICO. WE LIKE TO MIX JAMAICA WITH ORANGE JUICE AND SPARKLING WATER FOR A HIGH-C COCKTAIL.

Bring the water to a boil. Add the flowers and return to a boil. Reduce to a simmer and cook 10 minutes. Stir in the sugar or honey, strain into a pitcher and refrigerate. Serve cold over ice with slices of orange as garnish.

WATERMELON

WATERMELON JUICE

Makes 3 tall glasses

2 cups watermelon chunks, seeded

2 tablespoons sugar

1/2 cup cold water

5 ice cubes

juice of 1 lime (optional)

THIS REFRESHING, EASY-TO-MAKE, HEALTHFUL, BRIGHT PINK FRUIT JUICE IS A SURE CHILD-PLEASER. THE RECIPE WORKS EQUALLY WELL WITH CANTALOUPE, HONEYDEW OR OTHER RIPE MELONS. THIS IS A GREAT WAY TO USE LEFTOVER OR SLIGHTLY OVERRIPE MELON.

Combine all of the ingredients in a blender and puree until smooth. Serve over ice.

HORCHATA

Makes 3 quarts

1 quart nonfat milk

2 quarts water

4 cinnamon sticks

¼ cup rice flour or ⅓ cup raw white rice crushed to a powder in the blender

¾ cup sugar

1 tablespoon vanilla extract

HORCHATA, THE TRADITIONAL RICE DRINK OF MEXICO, IS A GOOD WAY TO SNEAK SOME ADDED NUTRITION INTO CHILDREN'S DIETS. WE LIKE IT WITH RICH STEWED MEATS, AS AN AFTERNOON PICK-ME-UP OR MIXED WITH KAHLÚA AS A COCKTAIL.

Pour the milk into a wide skillet and bring to a boil. Reduce to a simmer and cook, stirring frequently, until reduced by half, 20 to 30 minutes. Strain into a large saucepan and add the water and cinnamon sticks.

Bring to a boil, reduce to a simmer and cook 5 minutes. Remove from the heat and let sit 15 minutes. Remove the cinnamon sticks and reserve.

Combine the rice flour, sugar and vanilla in a bowl. Pour in the milk mixture and whisk to incorporate well. Refrigerate at least 4 hours. Then pour the liquid into a pitcher, discarding the sediment that has settled on the bottom of the bowl. Serve cold over ice, with cinnamon sticks as stirrers.

COCONUT LIQUADO

Makes 1 quart

1 small coconut

½ cup honey

3 cups milk

2 cups chopped ice

THIS COOL FRESH COCONUT MILK DRINK IS HIGH IN PROTEIN AND CALCIUM, NOT TO MENTION WORTH THE EFFORT.

Hammer a nail through each of the coconut's 3 eyes to puncture. Drain and reserve the milk. Crack and remove the hull by smacking it on its equator. Then, with a vegetable peeler, peel and discard the brown top layer. Break the meat into chunks and combine in a blender with the coconut milk, honey and 1 cup of the milk. Blend until smooth. Add the remaining 2 cups milk and the ice, and blend until the ice is finely crushed. Strain and serve in tall glasses over ice.

FRESH FRUIT LIQUADOS

Makes 1 quart

2½ cups chopped peeled ripe fruit, such as 1 banana plus 10 strawberries, 1 small cantaloupe, ¼ pineapple, 2 peaches or 2 kiwis plus 1 banana

1½ cups cold milk

2 cups chopped ice

3 tablespoons honey

LIQUADOS, THE EASY FRUIT-AND-MILK SHAKES OF MEXICO, ARE LIGHTER THAN MILK SHAKES AND HAVE THE ADDED VIRTUE OF BEING GOOD FOR YOU. VIRTUALLY ANY FRUIT CAN BE USED AS LONG AS IT IS WELL RIPENED (SLIGHTLY OVERRIPE IS PERFECT) AND ANY TOUGH SKINS OR SEEDS ARE REMOVED. THE ICE CAN BE CHOPPED IN THE BLENDER BEFORE COMBINING.

Combine the fruit with the milk, ice and honey in a blender or food processor and puree until smooth. Pour into tall glasses and serve immediately.

MEXICAN HOT CHOCOLATE

Serves 2

1 (3-ounce) tablet Mexican-style chocolate, roughly chopped

3 cups milk

MEXICAN DRINKING CHOCOLATE IS SWEETENED AND FLA-VORED WITH GROUND ALMONDS AND CINNAMON. IT MAKES A DELECTABLY RICH, FROTHY MORNING DRINK FOR CHIL-DREN AND OTHER CHOCOLATE LOVERS.

Place the chocolate chunks in a blender and pulse several times until broken into small pieces. Or grate by hand. Meanwhile, bring the milk to a boil in a small pot. Pour the hot milk over the chocolate, cover (with the vent open) and blend until thoroughly combined and frothy. Or whisk with a wire whip for 3 minutes. Serve immediately.

Hot Chocolate

COCKTAILS AND PEPITAS

SANGRITA

Makes 18 shots

2¼ cups freshly squeezed orange juice

¾ cup freshly squeezed lime juice

5 tablespoons grenadine syrup

1 generous teaspoon salt

1 teaspoon cayenne pepper

SANGRITA—A STRONG, SPICY, SALTY CITRUS DRINK MEANT TO ACCOMPANY STRAIGHT TEQUILA SHOTS—WILL BE WELL APPRECIATED BY TEQUILA LOVERS. THIS MIXTURE KEEPS IN THE REFRIGERATOR ABOUT FIVE DAYS.

Combine all the ingredients in a blender and process or whisk in a bowl until blended. Refrigerate. Serve cold in shot glasses with corresponding shots of tequila.

RED SANGRIA

Serves 4

4 oranges

1 lemon

1 lime

3 cups light, fruity red wine

2 cups ice cubes

USE INEXPENSIVE TABLE WINE TO PREPARE THESE CASUAL FRUIT AND WINE DRINKS—LIGHT AND FRUITY PINOT NOIR IS A GOOD CHOICE FOR THE RED AND CHARDONNAY FOR THE WHITE (SEE FOLLOWING RECIPE). THE ONLY TRICK TO SERVING THEM IS TO ADD THE ICE AT THE VERY LAST MOMENT, SINCE IT WILL MELT QUICKLY AND WATER DOWN THE WINE.

Cut 1 of the oranges, the lemon and lime into ¼-inch slices. Place in a pitcher, pour in the wine and let sit 1 to 2 hours. Juice the remaining 3 oranges. Just before serving, stir in the orange juice and ice cubes. Serve immediately.

WHITE SANGRIA

Serves 4

½ pound seedless green grapes, stems removed

1 to 2 Red Delicious apples, cored and thinly sliced

3 cups fruity white wine

1 cup apple juice

1 cup pineapple juice

2 cups ice cubes

THINLY SLICED PEACHES AND PEARS ALSO GO WELL IN THIS PRETTY WHITE SANGRIA.

Combine the grapes, apples and white wine in a pitcher and let sit 1 to 2 hours. Pour in the apple and pineapple juices, add the ice cubes and serve.

SPICY PEPITAS

Makes 2 cups

2 cups pepitas (raw hulled green pumpkin seeds)

1 teaspoon freshly ground black pepper

1 teaspoon cayenne pepper

1 teaspoon ground cumin

1 teaspoon ground ancho chiles or chili powder

1 teaspoon salt

2 teaspoons lime juice

KEEP PEPITAS OR RAW PUMPKIN SEEDS IN THE FREEZER TO MAKE QUICK COCKTAIL SNACKS FOR UNEXPECTED GUESTS. THEY DO NOT NEED DEFROSTING FOR THIS RECIPE.

Preheat the oven to 375°F.

Toss all of the ingredients together in a bowl. Spread on a baking sheet and bake 5 minutes, or until lightly browed, shaking the pan once or twice.

BORDER SUNSET

Serves 1

2 ounces gold tequila

½ cup freshly squeezed orange juice

½ cup Jamaica Flower Water, page 19

lime and orange slices

THIS STRIKING COCKTAIL HAS BRILLIANT LAYERS OF OR-ANGE, RED AND GOLD TOPPED BY FLOATING LIME AND ORANGE CIRCLES.

Pour the tequila into a tall clear glass filled with ice. Pour on the orange juice and then the Jamaica. Float slices of lime and orange on top and serve with a stirrer.

BORDER LEMON-LIME MARGARITA

Serves 1

1 lime, cut into 5 slices

margarita or kosher salt

2 ounces *añejo* tequila

1 ounce orange liqueur such as Triple Sec

1 tablespoon freshly squeezed lemon juice

½ coffee cup ice cubes

WE USE LEMON JUICE IN OUR MARGARITAS BECAUSE OUR LEMONS ARE CLOSER TO THE LESS ACIDIC LIMES FOUND IN MEXICO. THIS RECIPE CAN BE MULTIPLIED FOR LARGER GATHERINGS AND ADAPTED FOR UNBLENDED MARGARITAS BY SIMPLY COMBINING THE INGREDIENTS IN A MARTINI SHAKER AND THEN SERVING IN CHILLED GLASSES.

Arrange 3 lime slices on a small plate and cover another plate with the salt to a depth of ¼ inch. Place a martini glass upside down on the limes and press and turn to dampen. Then dip in the salt to coat the rim.

Combine the tequila, orange liqueur, lemon juice and ice in a blender. Blend at high speed until smooth. Pour into the prepared glass, garnish with the remaining lime slices and serve.

NOTE

TO MAKE 8 MARGARITAS, MIX 2 CUPS TEQUILA, 1 CUP TRIPLE SEC AND ½ CUP FRESHLY SQUEEZED LEMON JUICE. PREPARE IN 3 BATCHES; SHAKE OR BLEND A THIRD OF THE MIX WITH ABOUT 1 COFFEE CUP ICE FOR EACH BATCH.

1.

3 LIMES

2.

SALT

3.

Dips, Salsas,

Relishes and Pickles

OUR FIRST EXPOSURE TO SALSA-MAKING WAS IN THE

KITCHENS WHERE WE APPRENTICED. LATER, AT OUR

OWN CITY RESTAURANT, THE LATIN STAFF WOULD GRAB A FEW

TOMATOES, GARLIC, ONIONS AND CHILES OFF THE SHELF AND

WITHIN MINUTES HAVE DELICIOUS FRESH SAUCES FOR THEIR

LUNCH—WHILE WE WERE LABORING OVER PERFECTLY EMUL-

SIFIED, ENDLESSLY STRAINED FRENCH SAUCES FOR A LIVING!

SOMETHING SEEMED WRONG WITH THAT EQUATION.

Now we too are having fun mixing up casual quick salsas at the Border Grill. It seems almost antithetical to their casual nature to provide measurements. Once you get the knack, feel free to toss your own combinations (raw or roasted) into a blender, boil them down a bit (or don't) and sauce your foods the easy way, with fresh, delicious, homemade salsas.

As for the dips, relishes and pickles, they are salsa's spiritual cousins. They add a bright dash of color and exuberant flavor to anything they share the plate with.

DIPS

BORDER GUACAMOLE

**Makes 3 cups,
or 6 appetizer servings**

5 ripe avocados, preferably Haas

6 tablespoons chopped fresh cilantro

1 medium red onion, diced

4 jalapeño chiles, stemmed, seeded and finely diced

3 tablespoons freshly squeezed lime juice

1½ teaspoons salt

½ teaspoon freshly ground black pepper

shredded lettuce for serving

sliced tomatoes drizzled with Cracked Black Pepper Garnish, page 43, for garnish

STRONG, SIMPLE FLAVORS ARE THE KEY TO A TRULY GREAT GUACAMOLE. EVERYTHING MUST BE FRESH—ESPECIALLY THE ONIONS. WE PREFER TO USE TOMATOES JUST AS A GARNISH SO THEY DON'T WATER DOWN THE LUXURIOUS TEXTURE AND NUTTY TASTE OF PURE RIPE AVOCADO.

Cut the avocados into quarters. Remove the seeds, peel and place in a mixing bowl. Mash with a potato masher or fork until chunky. Add the remaining ingredients and combine with a fork. Mound on a bed of shredded lettuce and garnish with sliced tomatoes drizzled with the black pepper garnish. Serve immediately.

EULALIA'S CHIPS

Serves 8 to 10

3 cups Refried Black Beans, page 53, or good-quality canned refried beans

¾ cup Chipotle Salsa, page 34

8 ounces tortilla chips

1 cup Crema, page 249, crème fraîche or sour cream

1 cup grated *añejo* cheese

EULALIA, THE INCREDIBLE COOK AND HOUSEKEEPER OF A FRIEND OF OURS FROM LOS ANGELES, TOOK US UNDER HER WING ON OUR FIRST TRIP TO MEXICO CITY AND TAUGHT US THE WONDERS OF HER MEXICAN KITCHEN. ALTHOUGH THIS RECIPE DID NOT COME FROM HER, IT CAPTURES HER EARTHY SOPHISTICATION. THESE SWEET, SMOKY NACHOS, SIMILAR TO THOSE SOLD ON A BEACH WE HUNG OUT ON AT PLAYA DEL CARMEN, ARE TERRIFIC ADULT PARTY FOOD.

Preheat the broiler.

Spread the black beans in a ¼-inch layer on an ovenproof platter or casserole. Spread the chipotle salsa over the beans. Place under the broiler just to heat through, about 6 minutes.

Stand the tortilla chips, points up, in the beans. Using a plastic squeeze bottle, pastry bag or the tines of a fork, drizzle the crema, crème fraîche or sour cream over the chips. Sprinkle with the *añejo* cheese and return to the broiler for 3 to 5 minutes, until the cheese melts. Serve hot.

BLACK BEAN DIP

Serves 8 to 12

3 cups Refried Black Beans, page 53, or good-quality canned refried beans

¾ cup sour cream

2 teaspoons ground cumin (optional)

1 cup Salsa Fresca, page 40

Fried Tortilla Chips, page 129

THIS ECONOMICAL SOUR CREAM–BEAN DIP WAS INVENTED THE NIGHT WE RAN OUT OF GUACAMOLE AT THE RESTAURANT. NOW IT IS A STANDBY ON PARTY BUFFETS, WHERE ITS LURID PURPLE COLOR IS STRIKING NEXT TO GREEN GUACAMOLE AND RED AND GREEN SALSAS.

Place the beans in a food processor with the metal blade or a mixer with a paddle. Process or mix 2 to 3 minutes, until fairly smooth. Add the sour cream and cumin, if desired, and mix another minute to blend. Stir in the salsa fresca just until combined. Transfer to a serving bowl and serve with crisp fried tortilla chips.

SALSAS

Chipotle Salsa

Makes 6 cups

4 ounces (about 25 to 30) dried chipotle chiles or 3 cups canned chipotle chiles, stemmed

8 ripe Roma tomatoes, cored

12 garlic cloves, peeled

2 quarts water

2 tablespoons salt

½ teaspoon freshly ground black pepper

This earthy brown salsa, Susan's favorite, lends a typical Mexican smokiness and heat to any food it touches. At the restaurant we serve it with chips for munching and use it in our marinades, soups and salad dressings.

Combine all of the ingredients in a medium saucepan. Bring to a boil, reduce to a simmer and cook, uncovered, about 20 minutes. The liquid should be reduced by one-third and the tomato skins should be falling off. Set aside to cool.

Pour the mixture into a blender or a food processor fitted with the metal blade. Puree until smooth and then pass through a strainer. Serve chilled. Chipotle salsa can be stored in the refrigerator up to 5 days or frozen.

CHILE DE ÁRBOL SALSA

Makes 2 ¹/₂ cups

¹/₂ pound Roma tomatoes

³/₄ pound tomatillos, husked and washed

1 cup (30 to 40) árbol chiles

¹/₂ bunch cilantro, leaves only, roughly chopped

1 medium white onion, chopped

4 garlic cloves, crushed

2 cups water

1 teaspoon salt

¹/₂ teaspoon freshly ground black pepper

THE PEPPERINESS OF CHILES DE ÁRBOL IS BALANCED WITH SWEET TOMATOES AND TART GREEN TOMATILLOS. AN ASSERTIVE SAUCE SUCH AS THIS ONE GOES WELL WITH BEEF OR PORK—IT WOULD BE PERFECT UNDER A GRILLED RIB EYE STEAK—OR PORK CHOPS. AT THE RESTAURANT WE SERVE IT WITH CARNITAS, POSOLE AND CHIPS FOR CHILE LOVERS.

Preheat the broiler. Place the tomatoes and tomatillos on a baking sheet. Broil, turning occasionally, until charred all over, 10 to 12 minutes. Transfer to a saucepan along with the remaining ingredients.

Bring to a boil and cook until the onions are soft, 12 to 15 minutes. Transfer to a food processor or blender. Puree and then strain. Serve at room temperature or slightly chilled. Árbol salsa can be stored in the refrigerator 3 to 5 days or frozen for weeks.

SPICY COCKTAIL SALSA

Makes 1 cup

4 Roma tomatoes, cored and seeded

¹/₄ cup Chipotle Salsa, page 34, or 1 scant tablespoon Tabasco

¹/₄ cup freshly squeezed lime juice

1 tablespoon brown sugar

³/₄ teaspoon salt

¹/₄ teaspoon freshly ground black pepper

dash of Tabasco

THIS HOT COCKTAIL SALSA GOES WELL WITH POACHED SHRIMP, OCTOPUS OR RAW CLAMS. FOR A DELICIOUS VEGETARIAN STARTER, TRY SERVING IT WITH CHUNKS OF RIPE AVOCADO.

Place all of the ingredients in a blender or a food processor fitted with the metal blade. Puree until smooth. This salsa can be stored in the refrigerator up to 2 days. Serve cold.

RED TOMATO SALSA

Makes 1 1/2 quarts

2 tablespoons vegetable oil

1 medium onion, thinly sliced

4 cups diced canned Italian plum tomatoes

1 cup tomato juice

2 garlic cloves, peeled

1 large jalapeño chile, stemmed, seeded if desired

1 teaspoon salt

IF YOU ARE LOOKING FOR AN EASY SAUCE TO KEEP IN THE FREEZER FOR INSTANT MEXICAN MEALS, THIS IS THE ONE. IT PROVIDES THE FLAVOR BASE FOR SUCH TRADITIONAL DISHES AS TORTILLA SOUP, FIDEO, RED RICE AND CHILAQUILES AND CAN ALSO BE SERVED AS A SAUCE FOR STRONG, RICH FOODS—LIKE CHILES RELLENOS—THAT CALL FOR SOMETHING STURDY BUT NOT TOO ASSERTIVE IN THE BACKGROUND. WE USE IT AS ONE OF THE TRIO OF SALSAS ON THE TABLES AT THE BORDER GRILL FOR DIPPING CHIPS.

Heat the vegetable oil in a medium skillet over moderate heat. Cook the onions until soft, about 10 minutes. Transfer to a food processor fitted with the metal blade or a blender.

Add the remaining ingredients and puree, in batches if you are using a blender, until smooth. Pass through a medium strainer, pressing with a spatula or wooden spoon to push through as much pulp as possible. Pour into a saucepan, and add the salt. Bring to a boil, reduce to a simmer and cook, uncovered, 20 minutes. Adjust the seasonings. Set aside to cool for table salsa or use warm for red rice or chilaquiles. Store in the refrigerator 2 to 3 days or in the freezer for weeks.

ROASTED TOMATO SALSA

Makes 2 1/2 cups

1 pound Roma tomatoes

6 to 8 garlic cloves, peeled

1 to 2 jalapeño chiles, stemmed, seeded if desired

1/2 yellow onion, peeled

1 cup water

1 teaspoon salt

pinch of freshly ground black pepper

ROASTED SALSAS DEVELOP A DEPTH OF CHARACTER AND FLAVOR NOT USUALLY FOUND IN SUCH SIMPLE SAUCES. THEY GO EXCEPTIONALLY WELL WITH GRILLED MEATS OR FISH AND ARE ALSO NICE WITH SCRAMBLED EGGS AND WARM TORTILLAS FOR BREAKFAST. THE SIMPLE TRICK IS TO TRULY BLACKEN ALL THE VEGETABLES, EXCEPT THE GARLIC (WHICH SHOULD BE JUST GOLDEN), AND TO INCLUDE ALL THE JUICES FROM THE PAN IN THE PUREE.

Preheat the broiler. Place the tomatoes, garlic, chiles and onion on a baking tray. Tuck garlic under other vegetables to avoid blackening. Broil, turning frequently, until well charred, 15 minutes. Set aside to cool.

Transfer the roasted ingredients to a food processor fitted with the metal blade. Puree with the water until smooth. Season with the salt and pepper and serve. Store in the refrigerator 3 to 5 days or in the freezer for weeks.

Tomato

PUREED TOMATO SALSA CRUDA

Makes ³/₄ cup

4 Roma tomatoes, cored and cut into quarters

1 to 2 serrano chiles, stemmed, seeded if desired and sliced

juice of 1 lime

1 teaspoon salt

½ teaspoon freshly ground black pepper

ONE OF OUR FAVORITE SALSAS—IT'S SO EASY TO MAKE, AND IT'S A GREAT LIFESAVER WHEN YOU'RE UNEXPECTEDLY CALLED UPON TO PRODUCE A MEAL (OR A SNACK). IT'S GREAT WITH CHIPS AND QUESADILLAS OR AS A GARNISH FOR GRILLED FISH.

Combine all of the ingredients in a blender and puree until smooth.

TOMATILLO SALSA

Makes 3¹/₂ cups

1 pound tomatillos, husked, washed and cut into quarters

2 to 4 large jalapeño chiles, stemmed, seeded if desired and roughly chopped

½ cup cold water

½ medium onion, cut in half

2 bunches cilantro, stems and leaves

2 teaspoons salt

THIS TART, FRESH GREEN SALSA—ONE OF OUR BASIC TABLE SALSAS—IS INCOMPARABLE FOR CUTTING THE RICHNESS OF MORE COMPLICATED HOT AND SPICY FOODS, SUCH AS THE MUSHROOM EMPANADAS ON PAGE 71. AT THE RESTAURANT, WE COOK DOWN LEFTOVER TOMATILLO SALSA TO MAKE A SIMPLE GREEN SALSA TO ACCOMPANY FISH OR MEATS.

Place the tomatillos, jalapeños and water in a blender or a food processor fitted with the metal blade. Puree just until chunky. Then add the remaining ingredients and puree about 2 minutes more, or until no large chunks remain. This salsa keeps in the refrigerator, in a covered container, about 3 days.

ROASTED TOMATILLO SALSA

Makes 2 1/2 cups

1 pound tomatillos, husked and washed

6 to 8 garlic cloves, peeled

1 to 2 jalapeño chiles, stemmed, seeded if desired

1 large bunch cilantro, leaves only

3/4 cup water

1 teaspoon salt

pinch of freshly ground black pepper

HERE IS A GREAT EASY SAUCE FOR SUMMER BARBECUES. TRY SERVING A TART GREEN PUDDLE UNDER A PIECE OF GRILLED CHICKEN OR FISH OR EARS OF CORN.

Preheat the broiler. Place the tomatillos, garlic and jalapeños on a baking tray and broil, turning frequently, until evenly charred, 15 minutes. (The trick to keeping the garlic from burning is to tuck it under the tomatoes.) Set aside to cool.

Transfer the roasted ingredients to a food processor fitted with the metal blade. Add the cilantro and water and puree until smooth. Season with the salt and pepper and serve. Store in the refrigerator 3 to 5 days or in the freezer for weeks.

ANCHO CHILE SALSA

Makes 1 cup

4 medium ancho chiles, wiped clean, stemmed and seeded

1 cup freshly squeezed orange juice

2 tablespoons freshly squeezed grapefruit juice

1 tablespoon freshly squeezed lime juice

2 teaspoons salt

1/2 teaspoon freshly ground black pepper

2 tablespoons olive oil (optional)

DRIED CHILES AND CITRUS JUICES ARE A GREAT COMPLEMENT TO RICH, EARTHY BEANS. WE SERVE THIS COMPLEX-TASTING SALSA WITH OUR HEARTY VEGETARIAN RED BEAN STEW (PAGE 120) AT THE RESTAURANT AND LOVE IT WITH A BIG BOWL OF TURKEY CHILI OR ANY BEAN SOUP AT HOME.

Toast the chiles directly over a medium gas flame or in a cast-iron skillet until soft and brown, turning frequently to avoid scorching. Slice the chiles into 1-inch strips, then into a very fine julienne. Combine all of the ingredients in a bowl, mix well and let sit at least 30 minutes or as long as 2 hours before serving. Ancho salsa keeps a few days in the refrigerator.

SALSA FRESCA

Makes 2 cups, or 6 appetizer servings with chips

4 medium ripe tomatoes, cored, seeded and finely diced

¼ red onion, minced

2 jalapeño chiles, stemmed, seeded if desired and minced

1 bunch cilantro, leaves only, chopped

2 tablespoons freshly squeezed lime juice

¾ teaspoon salt

pinch of freshly ground black pepper

SALSA FRESCA, PROBABLY THE MOST POPULAR SALSA IN MEXICO, ADDS AN APPEALING FRESH NOTE TO ANY FOOD IT ACCOMPANIES. IF YOU USE ALL FRESH INGREDIENTS, YOU CANNOT GO WRONG WITH THIS SIMPLE, CLEAN SALSA. WE LOVE IT WITH CHIPS, QUESADILLAS, CHICKEN TACOS OR A GOOD GRILLED STEAK.

Combine all of the ingredients in a mixing bowl. Stir and toss well, and serve. Store in a covered container in the refrigerator no more than 1 day.

ROASTED PEPPER AND ACHIOTE SAUCE

Makes 3 cups

2 tablespoons olive oil

1 onion, thinly sliced

1 teaspoon salt

½ teaspoon freshly ground black pepper

4 red bell peppers, roasted, peeled, seeded (see page 11) and thinly sliced

2 poblano chiles, roasted, peeled, seeded (see page 11) and thinly sliced

2 cups Achiote Sauce, page 41

SWEET, SMOKY PEPPERS ADD ANOTHER DIMENSION TO FRA-GRANT ACHIOTE SAUCE. WE DEVELOPED THIS SAUCE FOR THE GUATEMALAN TAMALES ON PAGE 84.

Heat the oil in a medium skillet over medium-high heat. Sauté the onions with the salt and pepper until soft and golden, about 5 minutes. Stir in the sliced roasted peppers and achiote sauce, reduce the heat and cook just to heat through. Store in the refrigerator up to 3 days.

ACHIOTE SAUCE

Makes 2¹/₂ cups

1 tablespoon unsalted butter

1 onion, roughly chopped

3 garlic cloves, minced

1¹/₂ tablespoons tomato paste

1¹/₂ tablespoons achiote paste (see page 6), crumbled

2 tablespoons white vinegar

2 cups chicken stock

1 teaspoon salt

2 teaspoons cracked black pepper

ACHIOTE PASTE, AVAILABLE IN MEXICAN MARKETS, IS A BRIGHT ORANGE SEASONING PASTE FROM THE YUCATÁN, MADE OF GROUND ANNATTO SEEDS, OREGANO, CUMIN, CINNAMON, CLOVE, PEPPER AND ALLSPICE. IT SHOULD ALWAYS BE SAUTÉED FIRST TO RELEASE ITS FLAVOR WHEN MAKING A SAUCE. THIS RECIPE CAN BE ADAPTED FOR USE WITH GRILLED FISH BY SUBSTITUTING CLAM JUICE OR FISH STOCK FOR THE CHICKEN STOCK. THE PICKLED RED ONIONS ON PAGE 46 ARE A PERFECT GARNISH FOR ANY ACHIOTE-FLAVORED DISH.

Melt the butter in a medium saucepan over medium-low heat. Cook the onions until soft and translucent, 12 to 15 minutes. Stir in the garlic and tomato and achiote pastes and cook an additional 3 to 5 minutes, stirring frequently. Add the chicken stock, salt and black pepper. Bring to a boil, reduce to a simmer and cook, stirring and skimming frequently, 12 to 15 minutes. Add the vinegar and cook at end for 2 to 3 minutes. Puree in a blender or food processor. Store in the refrigerator 2 to 3 days.

Achiote
Condimentado
Yucateco

La Perla

ADOBO

Makes 1 1/2 quarts

12 ancho chiles, wiped clean

1/2 cup white vinegar

2 cups water

1/4 cup olive oil

2 medium onions, thinly sliced

5 garlic cloves, sliced

1 tablespoon ground cumin

4 cups chicken stock

2 tablespoons brown sugar

1/4 cup freshly squeezed orange juice

1/4 cup freshly squeezed lemon juice

2 tablespoons tomato paste

1 tablespoon salt

1/4 teaspoon freshly ground black pepper

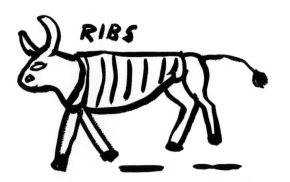

WE'VE BEEN EXPERIMENTING WITH ADOBO, THE SWEET AND SMOKY LATIN AMERICAN BARBECUE SAUCE, SINCE 1985 AND FIND THAT WE LIKE IT WITH JUST ABOUT EVERYTHING: CHICKEN, BRISKET, LAMB AND ESPECIALLY PORK. KEEP IT ON HAND FOR LAST-MINUTE BARBECUES. ALL MOST MEATS NEED IS ABOUT AN HOUR'S MARINATION IN THIS RICH SAUCE TO COME OUT A WINNER ON THE GRILL.

Toast the chiles directly over a medium gas flame or in a cast-iron skillet until soft and brown, turning frequently to avoid scorching. Transfer the toasted chiles to a saucepan and add the vinegar and water. Bring to a boil, reduce to a simmer and cook 10 minutes to soften.

Transfer the chiles and liquid to a blender or food processor. Puree until a smooth paste is formed, adding a tablespoon or 2 of water if necessary to thin. Set aside.

Heat the olive oil in a medium saucepan over medium-high heat. Sauté the onions until golden brown, 8 to 10 minutes. Stir in the garlic and cook briefly just to release the aroma. Then stir in the cumin and cook another minute. Add the chicken stock and reserved chile paste. Bring to a boil, reduce to a simmer and cook 20 minutes.

Meanwhile, mix together the brown sugar, orange and lemon juices, tomato paste, salt and pepper to form a paste. Add to the simmering stock mixture and continue cooking another 15 minutes. Adobo can be stored in the refrigerator 1 week or frozen indefinitely.

GREEN CHILE PASTE

Makes ¹/₂ cup

2 poblanos, roasted, seeded and peeled

¹/₂ jalapeño chile, stemmed, seeded if desired and roughly chopped

2 garlic cloves, peeled

¹/₂ bunch cilantro, leaves only

¹/₂ small red onion, peeled and chopped

1 teaspoon salt

juice of 2 limes

2 tablespoons water

2 tablespoons olive oil

A COMBINATION OF ROASTED AND FRESH TASTES MAKES FOR AN INTERESTING PLAY IN THIS SPICY PASTE. GREAT WITH GRILLED OR SEARED MEATS.

Combine all of the ingredients in a blender and puree until a chunky paste is formed. Serve at room temperature.

CRACKED BLACK PEPPER GARNISH

Makes ¹/₂ cup

2 tablespoons cracked black pepper

¹/₂ cup olive oil

2 tablespoons freshly squeezed lemon juice

1 teaspoon salt

THE PERFECT ACCOMPANIMENT TO A RIPE RICH AVOCADO. WE COULDN'T LIVE WITHOUT IT. USE ANY TIME YOU NEED A BURST OF FLAVOR—BUT NOT AS A VINAIGRETTE, AS IT'S TOO POWERFUL.

Stir all the ingredients together in a small bowl. Spoon over vegetables or drizzle lightly over dressed salads as a garnish.

RELISHES

CITRUS CUCUMBER RELISH

Makes 4 to 5 cups

7 pickling cucumbers, ends trimmed first
to remove bitter juices, then peeled

1 small red onion

6 Roma tomatoes, cored

1 cup shredded white cabbage

1 to 2 serrano chiles, stemmed, seeded if
desired and finely diced

1 cup freshly squeezed orange juice

¼ cup freshly squeezed grapefruit juice

2 tablespoons freshly squeezed lime juice

1 tablespoon salt

THIS CRUNCHY SWEET-AND-SOUR RELISH IS TERRIFIC ON SEAFOOD TACOS OR ACCOMPANYING SIMPLY GRILLED FISH OR POACHED SHELLFISH.

Cut the cucumbers lengthwise into thin slices, then into fine julienne. Halve the onion lengthwise, then slice into fine julienne. Cut the tomatoes in half lengthwise, remove the seeds and then julienne.

Place all of the ingredients in a bowl, combine well and let stand, covered, 30 minutes or longer. The juice will be salty and spicy, like fresh pickle juice, when ready. Store in the refrigerator up to 48 hours.

ONION RELISH

Makes ½ cup

2 small onions, finely diced

2 serrano chiles, stemmed, seeded if
desired and finely diced

½ cup red wine vinegar

¾ teaspoon salt

THIS IS A TRADITIONAL MEXICAN ACCOMPANIMENT FOR GRILLED STEAK OR EVEN FRESH OYSTERS.

Combine the onions, chiles and vinegar in a small bowl and let sit for an hour to marinate.

AVOCADO CORN RELISH

Makes 6 cups

¾ cup olive oil

4 cups fresh corn kernels (about 5 ears)

1 teaspoon salt

¾ teaspoon freshly ground black pepper

2 avocados, peeled and seeded

1 large red bell pepper, cored and seeded

4 poblano chiles, roasted, peeled and seeded (see page 11)

4 scallions, white and light green parts, thinly sliced on the diagonal

½ cup red wine vinegar

IN THIS REFRESHING RELISH, CORN KERNELS ARE LIGHTLY COOKED JUST TO DEVELOP THEIR FLAVOR AND THEN MIXED WITH CHUNKS OF SMOKY ROASTED CHILES, LUXURIOUS AVOCADO AND CRUNCHY SHARP SCALLIONS. SUCH A FABULOUS RELISH CAN EASILY TAKE THE PLACE OF A COOKED SAUCE WITH CASUAL FOODS LIKE GRILLED SKIRT STEAK OR FISH, AND IT IS A BOON ON BUFFET TABLES SINCE IT COMPLEMENTS SO MANY FOODS. WE HAVE BEEN KNOWN TO EAT CORN RELISH OFF THE SPOON OR WITH NOTHING MORE THAN TORTILLAS AND BE QUITE CONTENT.

Heat ½ cup of the olive oil in a large skillet over medium heat. Sauté the corn with the salt and pepper, about 5 minutes. Transfer to a large mixing bowl and set aside to cool.

Cut the avocados, bell pepper and roasted poblanos into ¼-inch dice.

Add to the sautéed corn along with the scallions, red wine vinegar and remaining ¼ cup olive oil. Mix well and let sit 20 to 30 minutes to blend the flavors.

Serve at room temperature. Corn relish can be stored, tightly covered, in the refrigerator up to a day. To make 2 to 3 days in advance, mix all the ingredients except the avocado and store in the refrigerator. Add the avocado shortly before serving.

PICKLES

PICKLED RED ONIONS

Makes 5 1/2 cups

1 pound red onions, thinly sliced

1 cup white vinegar

1 teaspoon cracked black pepper

1 teaspoon roughly chopped cumin seeds

1 teaspoon dried oregano

4 garlic cloves, sliced

2 tablespoons sugar

1 1/2 teaspoons salt

1 beet, trimmed, peeled and cut into 8 wedges

PICKLED RED ONIONS FROM THE YUCATÁN ADD A VINEGARY FLAVOR AND BRILLIANT PURPLE COLOR TO A WIDE VARIETY OF FINISHED DISHES. WE LOVE THEM WITH PANUCHOS, CHICKEN PIBIL, ANY GRILLED MEATS, AND ALL THE ACHIOTE-TINGED FOODS FROM THE YUCATÁN.

Place the onions in a medium saucepan and pour in enough water to cover. Bring to a boil, and remove from the heat. Strain and set the onions aside.

Combine all the remaining ingredients in the saucepan. Bring to a boil, reduce to a simmer and cook 10 minutes. Add the blanched onions and simmer an additional 10 minutes. Transfer the mixture to a container, cover and refrigerate at least a day before serving. Pickled onions will keep in the refrigerator up to a month.

PICKLED CHIPOTLES

Makes 2 cups

6 dried chipotle or morita chiles, stemmed, seeded if desired

2 cups red wine vinegar

WE COULDN'T COOK MEXICAN FOOD WITHOUT OUR TRUSTY JAR OF BROWN CHIPOTLES IN VINEGAR. THEY, AND THEIR JUICES, ADD A BEAUTIFUL SMOKY-SWEET, COMPLEX CHARACTER TO SALADS, STEWS AND SALSAS.

Combine the chiles and vinegar in a small pot. Bring to a boil, reduce to a simmer and cook, covered, 5 minutes. Set aside to cool. Store in a jar in the refrigerator up to 3 months.

PICKLED VEGETABLES

Makes 3 quarts

1 pound carrots, peeled and cut into
¼-inch slices on the diagonal

1 head cauliflower, trimmed and
separated into small florets

1 pound pickling cucumbers, unpeeled,
washed and cut into ¼-inch slices on the
diagonal

¾ cup chopped fresh oregano leaves

1 quart white vinegar

½ cup sugar

¼ cup coarse salt

2 tablespoons cracked black pepper

6 red jalapeño chiles

6 green jalapeño chiles

2 heads garlic, cloves separated, peeled
and cut in half lengthwise

1 medium yellow onion, sliced

THESE SPICY VEGETABLE PICKLES ARE COMMON ALL OVER
MEXICO AND ADD BRIGHT COLORFUL CONTRAST TO ANY
PLATE OR BUFFET.

Bring a medium saucepan of salted water to a boil, and blanch
the carrots for 3 minutes. Remove from the boiling water with a
slotted spoon, and refresh in a bowl of iced water. Drain and reserve. Then blanch the cauliflower about 6 minutes, drain, refresh
and drain again. Place the carrots, cauliflower, cucumbers and
oregano in a large nonreactive bowl.

Combine the vinegar, sugar, salt and pepper in a saucepan and
bring to a boil. Add the jalapeño peppers, garlic and onion and
return to a boil. Cook 1 minute longer, and pour over the vegetables.

Set aside to cool to room temperature. Pour into three 1-quart
glass jars and refrigerate as long as 1 month.

RED ↗ YELLOWISH GREEN ↙

JALAPEÑOS

Accompaniments

ONCE WE GOT BEYOND THE RICE, BEANS AND TORTI-
LLAS THAT ARE THE NATURAL ACCOMPANIMENTS TO
LATIN FOODS, WE THOUGHT DEEP AND HARD ABOUT OTHER
VEGETABLE SIDE DISHES FOR THE BORDER GRILL. THEY HAD TO
BE HIGHLY FLAVORED TO BE SERVED ALONGSIDE SUCH HEARTY
FOODS, EASILY PREPARED AND INTERESTING ENOUGH TO
STAND ALONE ON OUR POPULAR VEGETABLE PLATTER. ALL ARE
DELICIOUS, BUT WE ARE ESPECIALLY PROUD OF THE ROASTED
AND STEWED VEGETABLES LIKE FENNEL, GREEN BEANS, CAR-
ROTS AND CAULIFLOWER THAT CAN BE SERVED EITHER HOT OR
COLD AND HOLD UP EXCEPTIONALLY WELL TO ADVANCE PREP-
ARATION.

RICE, BEANS AND
OTHER BORDER BASICS

GREEN RICE

Serves 6 to 8

1 recipe Tomatillo Salsa, page 38

6 poblano chiles, roasted, peeled and seeded (see page 11)

5 romaine lettuce leaves

2 bunches cilantro, stems and leaves

4 scallions, white and green parts

6 garlic cloves, peeled

½ cup cold water

2 teaspoons salt

¼ cup vegetable oil

3 cups long-grain rice, rinsed (see page 51)

MEXICAN COOKS HAVE DEVISED TWO BOLD, FLAVORFUL VARIATIONS ON PLAIN BOILED RICE—GREEN AND RED RICE. FOR BOTH, THE GRAINS ARE FIRST SAUTÉED AND THEN BOILED WITH FLAVORFUL CHILE-SPIKED SALSAS. THE RESULTING GRAINS HAVE A WONDERFUL ROASTED AROMA AND INTENSELY RICH FLAVOR. WHITE, RED AND GREEN RICE LOOK BEAUTIFUL SERVED TOGETHER BUT IF YOU HAVE TO CHOOSE, SERVE GREEN WHEN YOU WANT A COOL ACCOMPANIMENT AND RED FOR A FULLER, SPICIER FLAVOR.

Preheat the oven to 350°F.

Pour the tomatillo salsa into a food processor or a blender. Add the poblano chiles, lettuce leaves, cilantro, scallions, garlic, water and salt and process until liquefied. (If using a blender, work in batches.) Set aside.

Heat the vegetable oil in a medium skillet over medium-low heat. Sauté the rice, stirring constantly, until golden and crackling, about 5 minutes. Pour in the reserved green puree and stir to combine. Transfer to a 4-quart baking dish, cover with foil and bake until the liquid is absorbed and the rice is tender, 30 to 35 minutes. Stir with a fork and serve hot.

CILANTRO

RED RICE

Serves 6 to 8

⅓ cup vegetable oil

3 cups long-grain rice, rinsed (see page 51)

1 medium onion, chopped

5 serrano chiles, or to taste, stemmed, seeded if desired

2 garlic cloves, chopped

¾ cup chicken stock, Vegetable Stock, page 115, or water

3 cups Red Tomato Salsa, page 36

Preheat the oven to 350°F.

Heat the oil in a medium heavy saucepan or skillet over medium-low heat. Sauté the rice, stirring constantly, until golden and crackling, about 5 minutes. Add the onions and serranos and cook until the onions just soften. Then add the garlic and sauté until the aroma is released. Pour in the stock or water and tomato salsa, mixing well to combine. Transfer to a 4-quart baking dish or casserole. Cover with foil and bake until the liquid is absorbed and the rice is tender, 30 to 40 minutes. Stir and serve hot.

WHITE RICE

Serves 4 to 6

2 cups long-grain rice

3 cups water

3 tablespoons unsalted butter

1½ teaspoons salt

½ teaspoon freshly ground black pepper

Place the rice in a large bowl (not a colander) and rinse under cold running water for 5 minutes. (If you use a colander, the starch remains on the rice, leaving it sticky.) Drain.

Pour the water into a medium saucepan, add the butter and bring to a boil. Stir in the rice, salt and pepper and bring back to a boil. Reduce to a simmer, cover and cook until the water is absorbed, about 20 minutes.

VARIATION

FOR MOROS, A BEANS AND RICE COMBINATION TYPICAL OF THE CARIBBEAN, MIX TOGETHER 2 PARTS WHITE RICE WITH 1 PART COOKED BLACK BEANS, AND HEAT.

WHITE RICE WITH FRIED PLANTAINS

**Serves 6 for breakfast or
as an accompaniment**

3 ripe plantains

4 tablespoons unsalted butter

6 cups hot cooked white rice

A BOWL OF RICE TOPPED WITH SLIGHTLY CRISP FRIED PLANTAINS MAKES A COMFORTING AND HEALTHFUL CHILDREN'S BREAKFAST. LOOK FOR BLACKENED SKINS—THAT MEANS THE STARCH HAS TURNED TO SUGAR—WHEN PURCHASING PLANTAINS, OR USE RIPE BANANAS.

Peel the plantains and cut into ¼-inch slices on the diagonal.

Melt the butter in a large skillet over medium heat. Sauté the plantains until golden brown and soft, about 2 minutes per side. Heap the rice on a platter and top with the browned plantains. Serve hot.

PLANTAIN

REFRIED BLACK BEANS

Serves 4 to 6

2 cups dried black beans, washed and picked over

7½ cups water

3 tablespoons lard or vegetable oil or 1½ tablespoons each unsalted butter and oil

1 large onion, diced

1½ teaspoons salt

DO NOT REDUCE THE QUANTITY OF FAT IN THESE RECIPES FOR FRYING BEANS: IT IS THE ABSOLUTE MINIMUM NECESSARY TO MASH THE BEANS TO THE PROPER LUSH CONSISTENCY. REFRIED BEANS FREEZE WELL.

Place the beans and water in a large pot and bring to a boil. Cover, reduce to a simmer and cook 1 hour, or until tender and creamy in centers. Crush the beans in their liquid with a potato masher or the back of a wooden spoon.

Heat the lard or other fat in a large saucepan over medium heat. Sauté the onions with the salt until golden, about 20 minutes. Add the beans and liquid and continue cooking over medium heat, stirring frequently, until the liquid evaporates and the beans form a creamy mass that pulls away from the bottom and sides of the pan, about 15 minutes. Serve immediately. Refried beans can be kept in the refrigerator 3 or 4 days and reheated in a covered casserole in a 350°F oven.

REFRIED PINTO BEANS

Serves 4 to 6

2 cups pinto beans, washed and picked over

2 quarts water

²/₃ cup lard or ¹/₃ cup (5¹/₃ tablespoons) unsalted butter and ¹/₃ cup olive oil

1 large onion, diced

1 teaspoon salt

¹/₂ teaspoon freshly ground black pepper

Pinto Bean

BLACK BEANS MAY BE FASHIONABLE THESE DAYS, BUT WE STILL LOVE A BEAUTIFUL BOWL OF PINK PINTOS TOPPED WITH FRESH CILANTRO AND CHOPPED ONION. BE VERY CAREFUL WHEN HANDLING BOILED BEANS IN THEIR BROTH. ALWAYS LET THEM COOL ENTIRELY, STIRRING THEM IN THE POT FROM THE BOTTOM UP OR TRANSFERRING TO A SHALLOW PAN SO THE STEAM IS RELEASED, BEFORE REFRIGERATING OR FREEZING. OTHERWISE, THEY CAN SPOIL RATHER QUICKLY.

Bring the water to a boil in a medium saucepan. Add the beans, reduce to a simmer, cover and cook, skimming occasionally, approximately 1¹/₂ hours. To test for doneness, taste 3 or 4 of the smaller beans. They should be cooked through and creamy inside. Mash, along with the liquid in the pot, with a potato masher or the back of a wooden spoon until creamy.

Heat the lard or other fat in a medium saucepan over medium-high heat. Sauté the onions with the salt and pepper until golden brown, about 10 minutes. Add the mashed beans and continue cooking, stirring occasionally, until the liquid evaporates and the beans form a mass that pulls away from the sides and bottom of the pan, about 10 minutes. Serve immediately. Refried beans can be kept in the refrigerator 3 or 4 days and reheated in a covered casserole in a 350°F oven.

SMASHED POTATOES

Serves 6

¹⁄₄ cup vegetable oil

6 medium Yukon Gold potatoes, peeled

coarse salt and freshly ground black pepper

¹⁄₂ cup Crema, page 249, crème fraîche or sour cream

THESE CRUSTY BROWN POTATOES WERE INVENTED ACCIDENTALLY ONE NIGHT WHEN WE DIDN'T HAVE TIME TO MASH. HAND CRUSHING PRODUCES THE KIND OF RUSTIC TEXTURE WE LOVE IN HOME COOKING.

Preheat the oven to 350°F.

Heat the oil in a cast-iron skillet over high heat. Cook the potatoes whole, turning frequently, until evenly browned, 10 to 15 minutes. Transfer to paper towels to drain.

When cool enough to handle, wrap each potato in aluminum foil and place in the oven. Bake until cooked through, about 40 minutes.

Remove the foil and transfer the potatoes to a serving platter. Place a kitchen towel over the potatoes and crush with the palms of your hands. Sprinkle with salt and pepper and garnish with the crema, crème fraîche or sour cream. Serve immediately.

SEARED GREENS

Serves 4

2 bunches red or green chard or mustard greens

4 tablespoons unsalted butter

½ teaspoon salt

freshly ground black pepper

THESE QUICKLY COOKED GREENS RETAIN ALL THEIR TART-NESS, COLOR AND VITAMINS. CHARD, ESPECIALLY, IS A GOOD REFRESHING ACCOMPANIMENT TO RICH, SPICY MEX-ICAN FOODS.

Trim and discard the stems of the greens and wash and dry the leaves. Stack the leaves, roll into cylinders and cut across the rolls into 1-inch strips.

Melt 1 tablespoon of the butter in a large skillet over medium-high heat until bubbly. Sauté one-quarter of the greens with ⅛ teaspoon of the salt and a pinch of pepper until the greens are limp, 30 seconds to 1 minute. If the greens begin to brown before they wilt, sprinkle in a few drops of water for steam. Transfer to a covered platter and repeat the procedure with the remaining 3 batches of greens. Serve immediately.

BORDER VEGETARIAN STARS

BRAISED FENNEL WITH MUSTARD GREENS

Serves 4 to 6

2 tablespoons olive oil

3 pounds fennel (about 3 large bulbs), tops removed and sliced crosswise into ¼-inch strips

1½ teaspoons salt

1 teaspoon cracked black pepper

½ cup white wine

1 bunch mustard greens, washed, stemmed and julienned

FENNEL'S PEPPERINESS IS ACCENTUATED BY BITTER GREENS AND WINE. YOU CAN DO MOST OF THE COOKING IN ADVANCE BY BRAISING THE FENNEL IN THE WINE FIRST. THEN JUST REHEAT AND ADD THE GREENS BEFORE SERVING. WATERCRESS, ARUGULA OR RED CHARD CAN BE SUBSTITUTED FOR MUSTARD GREENS.

Heat the olive oil in a large skillet over low heat. Add the fennel, salt and pepper. Cook, stirring frequently, until the fennel is light brown around the edges and soft, 15 to 20 minutes.

Pour in the wine. Turn up the heat and cook until the wine is evaporated, 8 to 10 minutes. Add the mustard greens and cook, stirring until wilted. Serve immediately.

FENNEL

BAKED YAMS WITH LIME AND HONEY

Serves 6 to 8

3 large yams (about 4 pounds)

1/2 cup water

6 tablespoons honey

4 tablespoons unsalted butter, at room temperature

juice of 4 limes

1 1/2 teaspoons salt

1/2 teaspoon freshly ground black pepper

Crema, page 249, crème fraîche or sour cream, for garnish

BAKING YAMS SLOWLY IN THEIR SKINS RETAINS ALL THEIR FLAVOR. WE CONSIDER THEM RICHER AND SWEETER THAN SWEET POTATOES. THIS DISH CAN BE COMPLETED AS MUCH AS THREE DAYS IN ADVANCE AND REHEATED. WE LOVE THESE RICH YAMS WITH GRILLED TURKEY BREAST WITH VINEGAR AND CRACKED PEPPER (PAGE 206).

Preheat the oven to 350°F.

Wash the yams and place in a baking dish with the water. Bake until the potatoes are soft and the skins puffy, about 1 1/2 hours. Set aside to cool slightly (leave the oven on).

Peel the yams and place in a medium baking dish. Add the honey, butter, lime juice, salt and pepper. Stir and mash well with a potato masher. Cover with aluminum foil and return to the oven for 15 to 20 minutes, until heated through. Sprinkle the top with crema, crème fraîche or sour cream and serve hot.

Stewed Green Beans with Tomato and Oregano

Serves 4 to 6

2 tablespoons olive oil

1 medium onion, thinly sliced

2 garlic cloves, thinly sliced

2 pounds green beans, ends trimmed

2 cups tomato juice

1½ teaspoons salt

½ teaspoon freshly ground black pepper

1 bunch oregano, leaves only, chopped

When you are lucky enough to have tender young green beans, simple steaming is the way to go. But when your beans are older, larger and tougher, stewing does a better job of softening and adding flavor. As with other stews, reheating only improves things.

Heat the olive oil in a medium skillet over medium-low heat. Cook the onion and garlic until soft, about 7 minutes. Add the green beans along with the tomato juice, salt and pepper. Stir well, cover and cook, stirring every 5 minutes, until the beans are tender and wilted, about 30 minutes. Stir in the fresh oregano and cook an additional 5 minutes. Serve hot.

ROASTED CARROTS
AND PARSNIPS WITH CUMIN

Serves 4 to 6

1 pound carrots, peeled and cut into ¼-inch slices on the diagonal

1 pound parsnips, peeled and cut into ¼-inch slices on the diagonal

3 garlic cloves, thinly sliced

2 tablespoons toasted cumin seeds (see page 12)

3 tablespoons honey

½ cup olive oil

⅓ cup water

½ tablespoon salt

¼ teaspoon freshly ground black pepper

juice of 2 limes

½ bunch mint, leaves only, chopped

TOASTED CUMIN SEEDS, MINT AND LIME JUICE INTENSIFY THE SWEETNESS OF THESE SIMPLY BAKED ROOT VEGETABLES. THEY CAN BE MADE A DAY OR TWO IN ADVANCE AND ARE EQUALLY DELICIOUS SERVED COLD.

Preheat the oven to 350°F.

Combine the carrots, parsnips, garlic, cumin seeds, honey, olive oil, water, salt and pepper in a medium baking dish. Toss well. Cover and bake for 20 minutes. Remove the cover and continue baking until the carrots begin to caramelize, about 20 minutes longer. There should be no liquid remaining in the pan. Sprinkle with the lime juice and mint and serve hot or cold.

BRAISED CAULIFLOWER WITH PARSLEY AND LIME

Serves 4 to 6

2 tablespoons olive oil

2 pounds cauliflower, cut into florets

1 teaspoon salt

¼ teaspoon freshly ground black pepper

1 bunch Italian parsley, leaves only, chopped

¼ cup freshly squeezed lime juice

SUSAN, A REAL CAULIFLOWER FAN, MADE IT HER MISSION TO CONVERT NONBELIEVERS WITH THIS WELL-BROWNED, CITRUSY SIDE DISH. IT IS ALSO DELICIOUS SERVED COLD.

Heat the olive oil in a medium skillet over high heat. Briefly sauté the cauliflower with the salt and pepper just to coat with oil, then reduce the heat to medium-low. Continue cooking, tossing frequently and adding a few tablespoons of water at a time as necessary to avoid burning, until the cauliflower starts to soften and brown evenly, about 35 minutes. Remove from the heat, stir in the parsley and lime juice and serve.

CREAMY RAJAS

Serves 6

¼ cup olive oil

2 medium onions, halved and cut into ¼-inch slices lengthwise

4 medium red bell peppers, roasted, peeled, seeded (see page 11) and julienned

4 medium poblano or pasilla chiles, roasted, peeled, seeded (see page 11) and julienned

1 cup heavy cream

¾ cup grated *manchego* or Monterey Jack cheese

⅔ cup grated *Cotija*, Romano or Parmesan cheese

THESE RAJAS, A TRADITIONAL ACCOMPANIMENT TO CARNE ASADA, ARE MEATY ROASTED PEPPER STRIPS, COATED WITH CREAM AND CHEESES TO TAME THE HEAT OF THE CHILES. THEY ARE DELICIOUS WITH GRILLED MEATS, POTATOES AND EGGS OR JUST WRAPPED IN WARM CORN TORTILLAS.

Heat the oil in a large skillet over medium heat. Sauté the onions with the salt and pepper until they begin to wilt and brown, 8 to 10 minutes. Stir in the julienned red peppers and chiles. Pour in the heavy cream, bring to a boil and reduce to a simmer. Cook 4 minutes or until the cream begins to thicken. Stir in the grated cheeses and remove from the heat. Serve immediately.

Pepper (Bell)

MASHED YUCCA

Serves 4 to 6

1¼ pounds fresh or frozen yucca

1 teaspoon salt

4 tablespoons unsalted butter

6 to 8 garlic cloves, minced

¼ cup white vinegar

½ teaspoon freshly ground black pepper

1 bunch Italian parsley, leaves only, chopped

YUCCA, OR CASSAVA, IS ONE OF THOSE UNUSUAL VEGETABLES THAT WE PREFER TO WORK WITH FROZEN SINCE THE QUALITY IS ACCEPTABLE AND IT'S NOT ALWAYS AVAILABLE FRESH. IT IS A STARCHY WHITE TUBER, SIMILAR TO A POTATO, THAT NEEDS STRONG FLAVORS LIKE GARLIC AND VINEGAR TO GIVE IT A BOOST. PEELED AND SLICED PAPER-THIN, YUCCA ALSO MAKES DELICIOUS FRIED CHIPS, BUT THEY MUST BE COOKED IMMEDIATELY ONCE SLICED.

Wash and peel the fresh yucca or thaw the frozen. Place in a small saucepan, and add water to cover and ½ teaspoon of the salt. Bring to a boil, reduce to a simmer and cook, covered, until tender, about 30 minutes. Drain in a colander and set aside to cool.

Preheat the oven to 350°F.

When the yucca is cool enough to handle, pull each root apart and remove the large fibrous veins near the center, keeping the flesh in large chunks.

Melt the butter in a large skillet over medium-low heat. Cook the garlic until tender but not brown. Add the vinegar, the remaining ½ teaspoon salt and the pepper. Bring to a boil and add the yucca. Stir and mash with a wooden spoon until a lumpy mixture is formed. Transfer to a baking dish. Cover and bake 10 minutes. Garnish with the chopped parsley and serve immediately.

STEWED CHAYOTE

Serves 6

6 chayote, peeled

1/4 cup olive oil

1 large onion, diced

3 garlic cloves, minced

2 tomatoes, cored, seeded and diced

1/2 cup water

CHAYOTE, A MILD-TASTING SQUASH, IS POPULAR IN MEX-ICO, WHERE IT IS OFTEN STEWED THIS WAY—WITH ONION, GARLIC AND TOMATO. WHEN BOILING SUCH A BLAND VEG-ETABLE, SALT IN THE BOILING WATER IS ESSENTIAL TO DE-VELOP FLAVOR.

Quarter the chayote and remove and discard the center seeds. Cut into 1/4-inch slices. Bring a large pot of salted water to a boil, add the chayote and boil for 5 minutes. Drain.

Heat the olive oil in a large skillet over moderate heat. Cook the onions until translucent, about 5 minutes. Then add the garlic and cook 1 to 2 minutes longer. Add the chayote, tomatoes and water. Bring to a simmer, cover and cook over low heat 10 minutes. Serve immediately.

CORN ON THE COB WITH CAYENNE AND LIME

Serves 6

6 ears corn, husked and cleaned

6 tablespoons unsalted butter

1 to 2 teaspoons cayenne pepper

juice of 2 limes (2 tablespoons)

1 teaspoon salt

FOR LARGE PARTIES WE LIKE TO CUT THE COOKED CORN INTO 2-INCH LENGTHS AND SERVE IT IN A COLORFUL BOWL.

Bring a large pot of salted water to a boil. Add the corn and cook just 4 minutes, no longer.

Meanwhile, melt the butter with the cayenne. Add the lime juice and salt. Drain the corn, toss with the cayenne butter and serve immediately.

SPICED PINEAPPLE LENTILS

Serves 4 to 6

3 tablespoons vegetable oil

2 onions, diced

1 teaspoon salt

1 teaspoon freshly ground black pepper

3 garlic cloves, crushed

2 cups lentils, washed and picked over

3 cups water

½ cup canned crushed pineapple

THESE RICH, SWEET LENTILS ARE LOVELY WITH THE BRAISED DUCK ON PAGE 208.

Heat the oil in a medium pot over moderate heat. Sauté the onions with the salt and pepper until golden, about 10 minutes. Stir in the garlic and lentils and cook 2 minutes, stirring frequently. Pour in the water, bring to a boil, reduce to a simmer and cook, covered, 45 minutes. Stir in the pineapple, remove from the heat and serve.

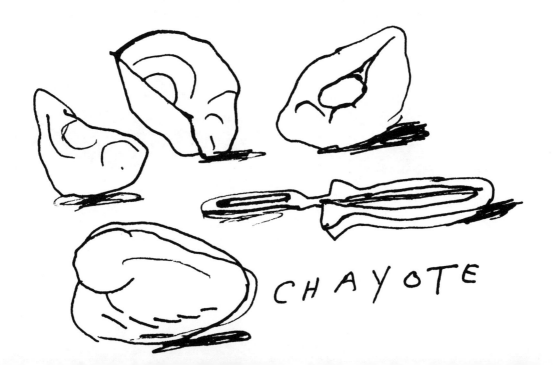

CHAYOTE

Stuffed Treats

These savory little treats should obliterate any unfortunate memories of tasteless bean dips and soggy taco casseroles. With their play of fabulous textures and tastes, they are party foods par excellence. If you enjoy serving something unexpected and truly special when you entertain at home, try a Mexican buffet of green corn tamales and plantain and mushroom empanadas. The food is guaranteed to capture at least as much attention as the perfect margaritas (page 26) and homemade fruit juices (pages 18–21) that accompany it.

CHILES RELLENOS

**Serves 6 as an appetizer,
3 as an entrée**

1 cup plus 2 tablespoons grated *manchego cheese*

1 cup plus 2 tablespoons grated *panela* cheese

¾ cup grated *añejo* cheese

6 large poblano chiles, roasted, peeled (see page 11), slit lengthwise down one side and seeded

flour for coating

4 large eggs

½ teaspoon salt

¼ teaspoon freshly ground black pepper

1½ cups vegetable oil

1 cup Roasted Tomato Salsa, page 37

1 cup Roasted Tomatillo Salsa, page 39

6 tablespoons Crema, page 249, crème fraîche or sour cream

FOR CRISP, FLUFFY STUFFED CHILES, THE LAYER OF FLOUR MUST BE JUST RIGHT, NEITHER TOO THIN NOR TOO THICK, WITH NO BARE SPOTS SO THE EGG BATTER ADHERES EVENLY—AND THE OIL MUST BE HOT. SINCE SIZES VARY, SUBSTITUTE TWO SMALL CHILES FOR EACH LARGE ONE AS NECESSARY. FEEL FREE TO OMIT ONE OF THE SALSAS FOR A MORE CASUAL PRESENTATION.

Combine the grated *manchego, panela* and *añejo* cheeses in a bowl and reserve.

Working on a towel-lined counter, spread open 1 chile at a time. Mold ½ cup of the cheese mixture in your hands to form a compact torpedo-shaped log and place inside the chile. Roll the flesh to entirely enclose the cheese, using the towel to help shape a tight roll. Place on a platter and stuff the remaining chiles. (They can now be reserved for up to 2 days, well covered, in the refrigerator.)

Preheat the oven to 350°F.

Spread the flour on a platter. Beat the eggs with the salt and pepper in a bowl wide enough for dipping.

Heat the oil in a 9-inch cast-iron skillet over medium-high heat until hot. Dip 3 chiles at a time in the flour, patting off the excess so just a fine even coating remains. Then place in the eggs.

Test the oil by dropping in a bit of egg. If it sizzles immediately and rises to the surface, the oil is ready. Drop the chiles, 1 at a time, into the oil, putting an extra dollop of egg batter on each. Fry 3 at a time until golden brown all over, about 1½ minutes per side. Drain on paper towels. Reheat oil and repeat with remaining chiles.

Transfer the chiles to a baking dish or tray and bake until the cheese thoroughly melts and heats through, 8 to 10 minutes. To serve, coat half of each serving plate with tomato salsa and half with tomatillo salsa. Top with 1 or 2 chiles and a dollop of crema, crème fraîche or sour cream. Serve hot.

ENCHILADAS FRESCAS

**Serves 6 as an appetizer,
4 as an entrée**

6 ancho chiles, wiped clean, stemmed
and seeded

2 cups water

½ cup white vinegar

4 garlic cloves, thinly sliced

1½ red onions, diced

1 tablespoon dried oregano

¼ teaspoon ground cumin

1 cup vegetable oil

12 large Corn Tortillas, page 132

6 ounces *panela* cheese, grated (1½ cups)

UNLIKE THE TRADITIONAL HEARTIER ENCHILADAS YOU MAY BE USED TO, THESE ARE LIGHT, THINLY SAUCED AND STUFFED WITH FRESH CHEESE. THEY MAKE A NICE VEGETARIAN FAMILY DINNER SERVED WITH RICE, BEANS AND WATERCRESS SALAD.

For the ancho chile salsa, place the chiles in a dry frying pan over moderate heat. Toast, turning frequently, until the skin blisters and darkens very slightly, 3 to 5 minutes. Remove from the heat.

Bring the water and vinegar to a boil in a medium saucepan. Add the chiles, remove from the heat and let soak 20 minutes to soften.

Place the garlic, half the diced onion, the oregano and cumin in a blender or food processor. Add the chiles and soaking liquid. Blend until smooth. The salsa may be made a day or 2 ahead and refrigerated.

Preheat the oven to 350°F.

Pour the vegetable oil into a large skillet and heat over medium heat. One at a time, dip the tortillas in the chile salsa and shake off any excess. Transfer the tortillas, one at a time, to the hot pan and sauté 10 seconds on each side. Drain on a rack.

Lay all of the tortillas out on a counter. Reserve ¼ cup of the grated cheese. Divide the remaining cheese into 12 portions and spoon onto the lower half of each tortilla. Divide the remaining diced onion evenly and sprinkle over the cheese. Roll up each tortilla to form a tube.

Arrange the enchiladas on a baking tray, seam side down, and bake 3 to 5 minutes or until heated through. With a spatula, transfer the warm enchiladas to a serving platter. Place about a spoonful of ancho chile salsa under each enchilada. Sprinkle with the reserved cheese and serve, passing the extra salsa at the table.

MUSHROOM EMPANADAS

Serves 4

3 tablespoons unsalted butter

1 onion, diced

1 garlic clove, minced

1 pound white or oyster mushrooms, cleaned and roughly chopped

1 1/2 teaspoons salt

1/2 teaspoon freshly ground black pepper

2 chiles de árbol, stemmed, seeded and finely ground, or 1/2 teaspoon cayenne pepper

1 bunch epazote or parsley, leaves only, roughly chopped

1 recipe Corn Tortilla dough, page 132

1 cup grated cheese mix (see page 9)

4 cups vegetable oil for frying

1 cup Tomatillo Salsa, page 38

1 cup shredded cabbage

1 cup Crema, page 249, crème fraîche or sour cream

WE FIRST TASTED THESE SAVORY LITTLE FRIED MASA TURN-OVERS IN OUR RESTAURANT KITCHEN, WHERE THEY WERE BE-ING PREPARED BY THE STAFF FOR LUNCH. WE PROMPTLY FELL IN LOVE WITH THE JUMBLE OF FLAVORS, TEXTURES AND ARO-MAS ENCLOSED IN SUCH A SMALL PACKAGE.

Melt 2 tablespoons of the butter in a medium skillet over medium heat. Sauté the onions until they just begin to brown. Then stir in the garlic and cook until the aroma is released, about 1 minute longer. Add the mushrooms, salt, pepper and árbol chiles. Continue cooking until the mushrooms soften, 5 minutes. Stir in the epazote or parsley and briefly cook just to release its flavor, about a minute. Set aside to cool.

Divide the corn tortilla dough into 16 equal balls and flatten to 1/4-inch-thick 3-inch circles, as directed on page 132. Divide the cooled mushroom mixture into 16 portions.

Lightly coat one side of each tortilla with the remaining softened butter. Place the mushroom mixture in the center and top with 1 tablespoon of the grated cheese mixture. Fold over to enclose and pinch the edges together tightly to seal. Refrigerate, covered with plastic wrap, a minimum of 30 minutes or up to 2 days.

Pour the oil into a medium saucepan and place over medium-high heat. When the oil is hot, fry the empanadas, a few at a time, until they color slightly and rise to the surface, about 7 minutes. Transfer to paper towels to drain.

To serve, split each empanada open along the seam and garnish with 1 tablespoon each salsa, cabbage and crema, crème fraîche or sour cream. Serve hot.

PLANTAIN EMPANADAS

Serves 6 to 8

3 ripe plantains, unpeeled

STUFFING

1 small poblano chile, roasted, peeled and seeded (see page 11)

1 cup cold Refried Black Beans, page 53, or good-quality canned refried beans

2 scallions, white and some green parts, thinly sliced

¼ cup grated *añejo*, Romano or feta cheese

¼ cup grated *manchego* or Monterey Jack cheese

¼ teaspoon salt

¼ teaspoon freshly ground black pepper

1 ripe banana, peeled

1 teaspoon salt

¼ cup peanut oil

1 cup Crema, page 249, crème fraîche or sour cream for garnish

IN THIS UNIQUE SOUTH AMERICAN SNACK—A FAVORITE AT THE RESTAURANT—A DOUGH OF SWEET PLANTAINS CONTRASTS BEAUTIFULLY WITH THE SAVORY BEAN AND CHEESE FILLING. THESE ARE GREAT FOR PARTIES SINCE THEY TASTE GOOD HOT OR AT ROOM TEMPERATURE, AND THEY FREEZE WELL. REMEMBER TO LOOK FOR BLACKENED SKINS FOR TRULY RIPE PLANTAINS.

Preheat the oven to 350°F.

Cut a lengthwise slit in each plantain and set on a baking sheet. Bake until the flesh is thoroughly soft and oozing through the slit, 40 to 50 minutes. Set aside to cool.

Meanwhile, make the stuffing: Finely dice the poblano chile. Combine with the remaining stuffing ingredients in a mixing bowl and stir to combine. The stuffing can be made up to a day in advance and reserved in the refrigerator.

Make the dough in a food processor or in a mixer with a paddle attachment: Peel, trim and discard any tough ends from the plantains. Combine the plantains, banana and salt and pulse until a smooth puree is formed, or mix until just blended. Be careful not to overwork the dough, or it will become too starchy. Wrap in plastic and chill about 2 hours.

To assemble the empanadas, roll 2 tablespoons of the dough lightly between your palms to form a ball. Line the bottom of a tortilla press with a small plastic bag and place the ball of dough in the center. Place another small bag over the dough and press to form a 3½-inch circle. (If you do not have a tortilla press, the dough can be flattened with the palm of your hand on a counter, with a sheet of plastic above and below to prevent sticking.) Place about 1 teaspoon of the bean stuffing on half of the dough circle and fold over to enclose, pressing the edges to seal. Place the stuffed empanadas on a platter and chill at least 30 minutes or as long as a day. (Stuffed empanadas can also be frozen.)

To cook the empanadas, heat the peanut oil in a medium skillet over medium-high heat. Fry 4 to 6 empanadas at a time, shaking the pan constantly, about 1 minute per side or until dark brown all over. (If they darken too quickly, as they may if very ripe plantains were used, lower the flame slightly.) Drain on paper towels. Serve hot with crema, crème fraîche or sour cream for dipping.

VARIATION

YOU CAN USE THE DOUGH AND FILLING TO MAKE AN EMPANADA PIE: DIVIDE THE DOUGH IN HALF AND PRESS HALF OF IT OVER THE BOTTOM AND SIDES OF A WELL-BUTTERED 9-INCH GLASS PIE PLATE. SPREAD THE FILLING OVER THE DOUGH. PRESS OR ROLL THE REMAINING DOUGH INTO A 10-INCH CIRCLE. PLACE OVER THE STUFFING, PRESSING THE EDGES TOGETHER TO SEAL. BAKE IN A 450°F OVEN FOR 15 MINUTES. CUT IN WEDGES TO SERVE.

EMPANADAS

CORN QUESADILLAS WITH CHEESE AND HUITLACOCHE

Serves 6

4½ tablespoons unsalted butter, softened

1½ medium onions, diced

3 garlic cloves, minced

6 ounces fresh, frozen or canned huitlacoche, thawed if frozen and drained

1 teaspoon salt

½ teaspoon freshly ground black pepper

6 large Corn Tortillas, page 132

1½ cups grated cheese mix (see page 9)

1 jalapeño chile, stemmed, seeded if desired and minced

HUITLACOCHE, A CORN FUNGUS CONSIDERED A DELICACY IN MEXICO, IS ONE OF THOSE UNIQUE FLAVORS LIKE EPAZOTE AND ACHIOTE THAT WAS A REVELATION TO US, EVEN AFTER ALL OUR YEARS IN THE KITCHEN. WE ALWAYS FIND IT WORTH THE TROUBLE TO SEEK OUT SUCH UNUSUAL INGREDIENTS TO KEEP OUR PALATES AND COOKING SKILLS GROWING. BECAUSE OF ITS UNUSUAL FLAVORS, THIS SIMPLE CORN TORTILLA DISH IS SATISFYING ENOUGH TO SERVE AS A SMALL MEAL.

Melt 1½ tablespoons of the butter in a small skillet over moderate heat. Sauté the onions and garlic until translucent, 6 to 10 minutes. Stir in the huitlacoche and stir for about 30 seconds. Season with the salt and pepper and set aside.

Preheat the broiler.

Place the tortillas on a counter. Coat one side of each with ½ tablespoon butter. Place one tortilla butter-side-down in an ovenproof 10-inch skillet, or place 2 or 3 in a broiler pan. Divide the cheese mix into 6 portions, and sprinkle cheese over the tortilla(s). Place under the broiler for 2 to 3 minutes to melt the cheese. Remove from the heat. Repeat with the remaining tortillas.

Divide the huitlacoche into 6 portions. Spread over the melted cheese and then sprinkle with the jalapeño. Fold the tortillas over to enclose the filling. Place the skillet over high heat and sauté the folded quesadillas two at a time, 1 minute per side, until slightly golden. Cut into quarters and serve immediately.

ZUCCHINI BLOSSOM QUESADILLAS

Serves 6

5 tablespoons unsalted butter

1/2 cup finely diced red onion

2 jalapeño chiles, stemmed, seeded and finely diced

1 pound zucchini or other squash blossoms, roughly chopped

1 teaspoon salt

1/2 teaspoon freshly ground black pepper

1 1/2 cups grated *manchego* or Monterey Jack cheese

1 cup grated *panela* cheese

1/2 cup grated *añejo*, Parmesan or Romano cheese

6 Flour Tortillas, page 134, or large Corn Tortillas, page 132

THE FLAVOR OF SQUASH BLOSSOMS, A TRADITIONAL FILLING FOR QUESADILLAS IN MEXICO, IS MUCH MORE COMPLEX THAN THAT OF THE VEGETABLES THEMSELVES. IF YOU ARE NOT A VEGETABLE GARDENER, YOU CAN FIND BLOSSOMS IN FARMERS' MARKETS OR MEXICAN AND ITALIAN MARKETS DURING THE SUMMER. CUT INTO WEDGES, THESE SPECIAL QUESADILLAS ARE EXCELLENT FOR A COCKTAIL PARTY.

Melt 3 tablespoons of the butter in a medium skillet over medium heat. Cook the onions and jalapeños until soft, about 5 minutes. Stir in the zucchini blossoms, salt and pepper. Reduce the heat to low and cook, stirring frequently, until the flowers are wilted, about 5 minutes more. Set aside.

Preheat the oven to 350°F.

In a bowl, combine the 3 cheeses. Lay the tortillas out on a counter. Divide the cheese mixture into 6 portions and arrange one portion over half of each tortilla. Divide the zucchini mixture into 6 portions and sprinkle evenly over the cheese. Fold over each tortilla to enclose the filling.

Melt the remaining 2 tablespoons butter.

Place a dry griddle or cast-iron skillet over medium-high heat. Brush one side of a quesadilla with melted butter and place buttered side down in the pan. Cook until very light golden, about 1 minute. Then brush the uncoated side with butter and flip over. Cook until the other side is golden, and transfer to a baking sheet. When all the quesadillas are browned, transfer the baking sheet to the oven and bake 10 minutes, until the cheese begins to ooze. Serve hot, whole or cut into wedges.

ROASTED GARLIC AND CARNITAS QUESADILLAS

Serves 6

1 tablespoon plus 1 teaspoon olive oil

2 large heads garlic

3 Flour Tortillas, page 134

1 cup Carnitas, page 136, slightly warmed or at room temperature

6 tablespoons grated *añejo* cheese

Green Chile Paste, page 43

THESE QUESADILLAS DERIVE THEIR RICHNESS FROM ROASTED GARLIC AND TENDER CHUNKS OF PORK, WITH JUST A SMALL SPRINKLING OF CHEESE TO BLEND THE FLAVORS. TO BALANCE SUCH RICHNESS WE LIKE TO SERVE THEM WITH A SHARP, SPICY SALSA LIKE GREEN CHILE PASTE.

Preheat the oven to 325°F.

Drizzle 1 teaspoon of the olive oil over each head of garlic and then wrap in aluminum foil. Place on a cookie sheet and bake 1 hour 15 minutes, or until soft throughout. Set aside to cool.

Reduce the oven temperature to 300°F.

When the garlic is cool enough to handle, slice each head in half across the width and squeeze the roasted garlic paste into a bowl, discarding the skins.

Lay the tortillas out on a counter and, with a spatula, spread a thin, even layer of garlic paste over the entire surface of each one. Divide the carnitas in thirds and spread over the bottom half of each tortilla. Sprinkle with the cheese. Fold over the top half to enclose the filling. Brush the top sides with the remaining 2 teaspoons oil.

Heat a griddle or dry cast-iron skillet over medium-high heat. Place a stuffed tortilla, oiled side down, in the pan and toast about a minute on each side, just to heat through. Keep warm on a tray in the oven while finishing the rest. Cut into wedges and serve immediately with the green chile paste.

CHEESE AND POBLANO QUESADILLAS

Serves 6

1½ cups grated *manchego* cheese

1 cup grated *panela* cheese

½ cup grated *Cotija* cheese

6 Flour Tortillas, page 134

⅓ cup Chipotle Salsa, page 34 (optional)

4 poblano chiles, roasted, peeled, seeded
(see page 11) and julienned

2 tablespoons unsalted butter, melted

TRY USING HOMEMADE FLOUR TORTILLAS FOR THESE TRA-
DITIONAL QUESADILLAS AND YOU WILL BE AMAZED AT THE
DIFFERENCE IT MAKES. THESE ARE GREAT PARTY PLEASERS
SERVED BY THEMSELVES OR WITH ROASTED TOMATILLO
SALSA (PAGE 39).

In a bowl, mix together the cheeses.

Lay the tortillas on a counter. Divide the cheese mix into 6 portions and spread over half of each tortilla. If desired, sprinkle about
a tablespoon of salsa over each. Arrange the chile strips evenly over
the cheese. Fold the tortillas over to enclose the filling and brush
the tops with butter.

Preheat the oven to 350°F.

Place a dry griddle or cast-iron skillet over medium-high heat.
Place the tortillas buttered side down in the pan. Cook until very
light golden, about 1 minute. Then brush the uncoated sides with
butter and flip over. Cook until golden, and transfer to a baking
sheet. When all the quesadillas are cooked, transfer the baking
sheet to the oven and bake 10 minutes, until the cheese begins to
ooze. Serve hot, whole or cut into wedges.

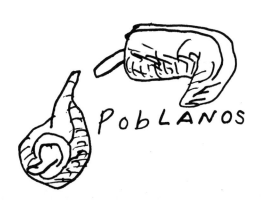
POBLANOS

Panuchos

Serves 6

½ recipe Masa, page 80

¼ cup Refried Black Beans page 53, or good-quality canned refried beans, pureed

about ⅔ cup vegetable oil

2 cups shredded roasted chicken (see page 195)

1 cup Roasted Tomato Salsa, page 37

1 cup Pickled Red Onions, page 46

1 avocado, peeled, seeded and sliced, for garnish

WE FIRST TASTED THIS FAVORITE FOOD IN THE VALLADOLID MARKETPLACE IN THE YUCATÁN. FRESH CORN TORTILLAS ARE DELICATELY SPLIT OPEN AND STUFFED WITH A THIN LAYER OF BLACK BEANS, THEN LIGHTLY FRIED AND TOPPED WITH SHREDDED CHICKEN OR TURKEY AND PICKLED RED ONIONS. THE TECHNIQUE MAY TAKE SOME PRACTICE, BUT THE RESULTS ARE WELL WORTH THE EFFORT.

Divide the masa into 12 pieces and form each into a ball. Press or roll each into a 4-inch circle, as described on page 132.

Heat a dry cast iron-skillet or griddle over medium-high heat and cook the tortillas as directed on page 132.

When cool enough to handle, pick up each puffed tortilla and make a 1½-inch slit about ¼-inch from the edge to make a pocket, being careful not to cut all the way through the tortilla. Stuff 2 teaspoons of the bean puree in each pocket. Flatten to seal and spread the beans evenly. Reserve the stuffed tortillas on a tray covered with a barely damp cloth.

Heat 3 tablespoons of the oil in a large skillet over high heat. Fry the stuffed tortillas in batches, adding more oil as necessary, until they are a little crisp around the edges but still pliable. Drain on paper towels. Then place on a tray and keep warm in a 200°F oven.

Heat the chicken in a small pan over low heat.

Remove the tray of panuchos from the oven. Top each with a scant tablespoon of roasted tomato salsa. Sprinkle on the chicken and pickled onions and top each with a small avocado slice. Serve warm or at room temperature.

VARIATION

IN CASE YOUR TORTILLAS DO NOT PUFF, HERE IS AN ALTERNATIVE PLAN: FRY THEM AS IS IN THE OIL, AND THEN SPREAD WITH A VERY FINE LAYER OF BEANS FOLLOWED BY THE OTHER INGREDIENTS. THEY WILL STILL TASTE DELICIOUS.

CHEESE AND GREEN CHILE TAMALES

**Makes 12 to 16 tamales, or
12 to 16 appetizer servings**

MASA

1 pound ground masa for tamales

½ pound lard, clarified butter or
vegetable shortening

4 poblano chiles, roasted, peeled and
seeded (see page 11)

⅓ cup Tomatillo Salsa, page 38

1 cup chicken stock, cold or at room
temperature

1 teaspoon baking soda

2 tablespoons salt

STUFF YOUR TAMALES AS GENEROUSLY AS POSSIBLE AND
DON'T WORRY ABOUT EXCESS STUFFING OOZING OUT. IT
WILL STICK TO THE OUTSIDE OF THE HUSK, DOING NO REAL
DAMAGE TO THE PRESENTATION OR TASTE. THIS RECIPE CAN
BE SPLIT UP BY PREPARING THE STUFFING A DAY IN ADVANCE.

Place the masa and lard or other shortening in separate contain-
ers in the freezer for 30 to 40 minutes, until cold but not frozen.

Combine the roasted poblanos and tomatillo salsa in a blender
or food processor. Puree until smooth and set aside.

Mix together the chicken stock, baking soda, and salt and set
aside.

When the masa is cold enough, empty into the bowl of a heavy-
duty mixer with a paddle. Beat on medium speed until the masa is
light in texture, 5 to 7 minutes. Turn the speed up to medium-high
and drizzle in the chicken stock mixture.

Remove the lard or other fat from the freezer. Turn the mixer
speed up to high, and add 1 tablespoon of fat at a time, making
sure each spoonful is incorporated before making the next addition.
Continue beating until the mixture is light and fluffy, about 15
minutes total. Test for lightness by dropping 1 tablespoon of masa
into cold water: If it floats, the mixture is light enough. If not, continue beating at high speed a few minutes longer.

Add the pureed chile mixture to the masa, and mix well to combine. Reserve at room temperature.

STUFFING

8 poblano chiles, roasted, peeled, seeded (see page 11) and diced

½ cup Tomatillo Salsa, page 38

1 teaspoon salt

3 packages dried corn husks, separated and soaked in hot water at least 2 hours or overnight

1½ pounds *panela* cheese, cut into ¼-inch cubes

1 recipe Tomatillo Salsa, page 38

To make the stuffing, mix together the poblanos, ½ cup tomatillo salsa, and salt.

To make the tamales, spread 1 large or 2 small softened corn husks on a counter, with the narrow end pointing away from you. Leaving about 2 inches bare at the top, spread a ½-inch layer of masa over the center and one side of the husk. Divide the poblano mixture evenly and sprinkle over the portion of masa in the center of the husk. Top the chiles with some of the cubed cheese.

Fold the side covered with masa over the chiles and cheese, and then fold over the other side to enclose. Fold down the top flap. Place the folded tamale on a large square of aluminum foil and wrap to enclose. Repeat with the remaining ingredients.

Line a steamer or a pot fitted with a rack with corn husks. Cook over simmering water 45 minutes, or until the corn husks can be pulled away from the masa without sticking. Serve hot with Tomatillo Salsa.

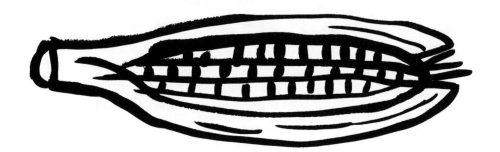

GREEN CORN TAMALES

**Makes 10 to 12 tamales,
or 6 servings**

10 ears corn

2 tablespoons unsalted butter

½ teaspoon salt

¼ teaspoon ground white pepper

pinch of sugar, if necessary

½ cup heavy cream

½ teaspoon baking powder

½ cup hominy grits

1 recipe Salsa Fresca, page 40

sour cream for serving

IF YOU ARE NEW TO TAMALES, THESE MILD CORN AND CREAM PACKAGES ARE THE PERFECT PLACE TO BEGIN. THERE IS SOMETHING UNIVERSALLY APPEALING ABOUT THEM (THEY HAVE BEEN STEADY SELLERS AT THE RESTAURANT SINCE 1985), AND THEY ARE NOT TOO DEMANDING IN THE KITCHEN EITHER. IN MEXICO, WHERE CORN IS THE STAPLE CROP, GREEN CORN MEANS FRESH RATHER THAN DRIED. IF FRESH CORN IS UNAVAILABLE, SUBSTITUTE THREE CUPS CANNED CORN CHOPPED IN THE FOOD PROCESSOR AND PURCHASE DRIED CORN HUSKS, OR *HOJAS*, IN A LATIN MARKET.

Remove the corn husks by trimming off both ends of the cobs, trying to keep the husks whole. Place the largest husks in a pot of hot water and set aside to soak.

To make the stuffing: working over a bowl, run the point of a sharp knife down the center of each row of kernels, and then scrape with the dull side to remove the kernels.

Melt the butter in a large skillet over moderate heat. Add the corn and its juices, the salt, pepper, the sugar if the corn isn't sweet and the cream and simmer until the mixture thickens, 5 to 8 minutes. Set aside to cool. Then stir in the baking powder and grits and reserve in the refrigerator.

Drain the corn husks on paper towels. Make ties for the tamales by cutting a few of the husks into strips.

To stuff the tamales, overlap 2 or 3 husks and spread about 3 tablespoons of corn filling down the center. Fold over the sides and then the ends to enclose the filling. Tie with a corn husk string. Repeat with the remaining filling and additional corn husks.

In a steamer or a pot fitted with a rack, make a bed for the tamales with the remaining corn husks. Add the tamales and steam over low heat for 1 hour. Remove from the steamer and let rest 10 minutes. Serve hot with the salsa fresca and sour cream.

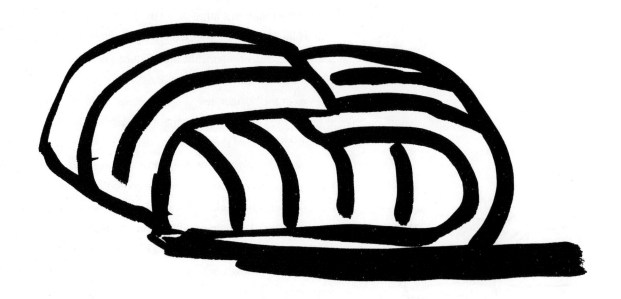

GUATEMALAN TAMALES

**Makes 6 to 8 tamales,
or 6 to 8 hearty appetizer or
light entrée servings**

MASA

1 pound ground masa for tamales

1 cup lard, vegetable shortening or clarified butter

3 tablespoons Achiote Sauce, page 41

1 cup strong chicken stock

1 teaspoon baking soda

1 tablespoon salt

IN THESE SUCCULENT TAMALES, FLUFFY MASA IS ENRICHED WITH RAISINS, OLIVES, CHICKEN AND A GENEROUS HELPING OF ACHIOTE SAUCE. SOFT, FRAGRANT BANANA LEAVES, AVAILABLE IN LATIN MARKETS, ARE THE TYPICAL TAMALE WRAPPER IN THE SOUTHERN MEXICAN STATES AND CENTRAL AMERICA. THESE WOULD MAKE A NICE HOLIDAY MEAL.

Make the masa according to the instructions on page 80, substituting the achiote sauce for the poblano mixture.

½ cup chicken stock

1 cup golden raisins

8 9-inch squares banana leaf, center stalk removed

1½ cups shredded roasted chicken (see page 195)

1 cup pitted green olives, sliced

1 cup Achiote Sauce, page 41

1 recipe Roasted Pepper and Achiote Sauce, page 40

Combine the chicken stock and raisins in a small saucepan and place over medium heat for about 3 minutes to plump. Drain and set aside.

Briefly hold each piece of banana leaf over a low burner just to soften. Spread a thin layer of masa over the center third of each leaf's shiny side. Sprinkle the chicken over the masa and top with the raisins, olives and achiote sauce. Fold to enclose and then wrap in aluminum foil according to the instructions on page 83.

Stack in a steamer and cook over simmering water 1 hour 20 minutes, or until the masa is just set and pulls away from the banana leaves. Remove and discard the foil and unwrap the tamales. Serve in the banana leaves with the roasted pepper sauce ladled across the top.

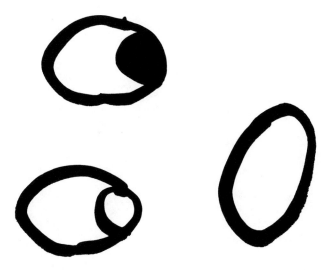

Marinated Openers

Some of the best seafood in Mexico can be found along the coast at the small beach shacks and sidewalk stands specializing in ceviches, or marinated fish salads. There you can watch the fish being caught and bought, skinned, filleted and turned into some of the most vibrantly refreshing fast food imaginable. We love the immediacy of such raw, strong flavors.

OYSTER COCKTAIL

Serves 4

24 raw oysters in the shell, scrubbed

1½ cups Spicy Cocktail Salsa, page 35

1 red onion, diced

1 bunch cilantro, stems trimmed and chopped

1 lime, quartered

4 Fried Tortilla Chips, page 129, for garnish

THIS SMOKY-HOT COCKTAIL SAUCE IS A FABULOUS ACCOMPANIMENT TO THE WIDE VARIETY OF RAW SEAFOOD AVAILABLE IN MEXICO'S POPULAR SEAFOOD BARS. IT IS EQUALLY DELICIOUS WITH CLAMS, SHRIMP, OCTOPUS AND SQUID. IF YOU DON'T FEEL LIKE MAKING OYSTER COCKTAILS, SERVE THIS BRACING SALSA ON OYSTERS ON THE HALF-SHELL OR IN SHOT GLASSES.

Place 4 martini glasses or wine goblets in the refrigerator.

Shuck the oysters. Place 6 oysters, with their juice, in each chilled glass. (Fresh, cleaned oysters can be reserved in the refrigerator for up to 6 hours.) Spoon the salsa into the glasses. Stir to combine. Sprinkle with the chopped onion and cilantro and serve with squeezed lime wedges and fried tortilla chips.

Oysters on the Half Shell with Chunky Tomatillo Salsa

Serves 2

12 raw oysters in the shell, scrubbed

4 tomatillos, husked, washed and very finely diced

2 scallions, white and some green parts, thinly sliced on the diagonal

1 bunch cilantro, stems trimmed and roughly chopped

1 tablespoon minced seeded jalapeño chile, seeds optional

½ teaspoon salt

½ teaspoon freshly ground black pepper

¼ cup freshly squeezed lime juice

2 tablespoons olive oil

WE LOVE THE CONTRAST BETWEEN THE SMOOTH WHITE OYSTERS AND CRUNCHY BRIGHT GREENS IN THIS RUSTIC UNCOOKED DISH. IT'S LIKE BITING INTO AN OYSTER TOPPED WITH ITS OWN LITTLE SALAD. THE CHUNKY SALSA ALSO GOES WELL UNDER A GRILLED FISH FILLET.

Shuck the oysters, reserving the juices. Place the oysters with their juice on 12 cleaned shells on a platter. Reserve in the refrigerator.

Mix together the remaining ingredients in a bowl. Cover with plastic wrap and chill at least 30 minutes or up to 4 hours to marry the flavors.

Spoon the salsa over the oysters and serve.

SHRIMP CEVICHE

**Serves 4 to 6 as an appetizer
(makes enough for 12 tacos)**

4 cups fish stock or clam juice

1 pound peeled rock shrimp or 1¼
pounds small shrimp, shell on

1 small red onion, finely diced

1 to 2 serrano chiles, stemmed, seeded if
desired and finely chopped

2 large bunches cilantro, stems trimmed
and roughly chopped

¼ cup freshly squeezed lime juice

1 teaspoon salt

THIS SIMPLE CEVICHE IS A GOOD CHOICE FOR ENTERTAINING SINCE THE FISH IS PARTLY PRECOOKED, ELIMINATING ANY QUALMS GUESTS MIGHT HAVE ABOUT RAW FISH. WE LIKE TO SERVE IT IN CHILLED CLEAR GLASSES ADORNED WITH A LARGE FRIED TORTILLA CHIP, OR ON A BED OF LETTUCE GARNISHED WITH SLICED AVOCADO FOR MORE FORMAL PRESENTATIONS. ROCK SHRIMP IS AN EXCEPTIONALLY SWEET, CRUNCHY, HARD-SHELLED SHRIMP THAT IS AVAILABLE FROZEN, SHELL OFF, IN SOME SPECIALTY MARKETS. OTHER SMALL SHRIMP CAN ALWAYS BE SUBSTITUTED.

Bring the stock or clam juice to a boil in a large saucepan or stockpot. Add the shrimp and cook 30 seconds for rock shrimp, 1 minute for shrimp in the shell. (For the marinade to really soak into the shrimp and the texture to remain crisp rather than rubbery, resist any temptation to overcook.) Strain, reserving the liquid, and spread the shrimp on a baking sheet to cool. When cool enough to handle, peel the shrimp if necessary.

Combine all of the remaining ingredients with the shrimp and 1 cup of the reserved cooking liquid in a bowl and mix well. Cover with plastic and chill thoroughly before serving.

VARIATION

TO ADAPT FOR FRESH FISH, MARINATE ¾ POUND OF SEA BASS OR SNAPPER FILLETS, CUT IN CHUNKS, IN ½ CUP FRESHLY SQUEEZED LIME JUICE UNTIL OPAQUE. DRAIN AND DISCARD THE JUICE. COMBINE THE FISH WITH 1 CUP CLAM JUICE AND THE REMAINING MARINADE INGREDIENTS LISTED ABOVE, WITH AN ADDITIONAL TABLESPOON OR TWO OF LIME JUICE.

OCTOPUS CEVICHE

Serves 6

1½ pounds raw baby octopus or cooked octopus meat

coarse salt for sprinkling

1 quart fish stock or clam juice

2 cups water

½ cup white vinegar

2 tablespoons black peppercorns

10 bay leaves

2 medium carrots, peeled and diced

2 small poblano chiles, stemmed, seeded and diced

2 small red bell peppers, cored, seeded and diced

½ cup fish stock or clam juice, if using cooked octopus

½ cup red wine vinegar

½ cup extra virgin olive oil

1 teaspoon salt

½ teaspoon freshly ground black pepper

Fried Tortilla Chips, page 129, for garnish

WE LIKE TO USE PLENTY OF CHOPPED, RAW VEGETABLES IN OUR FISH SALADS FOR A MEDLEY OF COLOR, TEXTURE AND FLAVOR. THE OCTOPUS CAN BE POACHED IN ADVANCE AND HELD IN THE REFRIGERATOR FOR A DAY, AND THE SAME MARINADE CAN ALSO BE USED FOR SQUID OR SHRIMP.

If using raw octopus, remove and discard the eyes and beak and clean thoroughly. Sprinkle all over with salt and knead well to tenderize. Rinse under cold running water.

To make the poaching liquid, pour the fish stock or clam juice, water and vinegar into a stockpot into which a large strainer can fit. Add the black peppercorns and bay leaves and bring to a boil.

Place the cleaned octopus in the strainer and dip in the boiling liquid for 30 seconds. Then remove and let rest about 2 minutes. Repeat this procedure twice. Transfer the blanched octopus to a tray and refrigerate until cold. Strain the poaching liquid and reserve ½ cup. Cut the octopus meat into bite-sized pieces, and refrigerate. (If using cooked octopus meat, just cut into bite-sized pieces.)

Bring a medium saucepan of salted water to a boil. Blanch the diced carrots for 4 to 5 minutes, drain and plunge into a bowl of iced water. Drain again and dry thoroughly.

Combine the chilled octopus with the carrots, chiles and red peppers in a bowl. Add the reserved poaching liquid or the fish stock or clam juice and the remaining ingredients and mix well. Chill at least 30 minutes before serving. (Finished ceviche can be kept in the refrigerator 1 day.) Serve in tall chilled glasses with the tortilla chips as garnish.

SWORDFISH CEVICHE

Serves 4 to 6

12 ounces swordfish, skin and dark meat removed

1 cup plus 1 tablespoon freshly squeezed lime juice

1 small red onion, diced

2 medium tomatoes, cored, seeded and diced

1/2 cup freshly squeezed orange juice

1/2 cup tomato juice

1 1/2 jalapeño chiles, stemmed, seeded and finely chopped

1 bunch oregano, leaves only, chopped

1/4 cup olive oil

1/2 cup small green olives

1 teaspoon salt

1/2 teaspoon freshly ground black pepper

3 bay leaves

4 to 6 lettuce leaves for serving (optional)

Fried Tortilla Chips, page 129, for garnish

UNTIL WE TASTED STRONG CEVICHES SUCH AS THIS ONE IN THE COASTAL CITY OF VERACRUZ, WE ONLY KNEW ABOUT USING FLAKIER FISHES, SUCH AS SNAPPER, FOR RAW FISH SALADS. NOW WE PREFER FIRMER FISH LIKE SWORDFISH WITH A FULL-FLAVORED MARINADE. ALTHOUGH TUNA IS OFTEN SUBSTITUTED IN COOKED DISHES FOR SWORDFISH, DO NOT USE IT FOR CEVICHE; THE MEAT WILL BECOME TOO DRY.

Cut the swordfish into 1/2-inch squares. Combine the fish and the 1 cup lime juice in a nonmetallic container, and marinate 30 minutes in the refrigerator. Drain and discard the lime juice. Transfer the fish to a bowl.

Add the 1 tablespoon lime juice and the remaining ingredients, toss well and chill at least an hour or as long as overnight. Remove the bay leaves. Serve cold in chilled glasses or on lettuce-lined plates, with crispy fried tortilla chips as garnish.

OAXACAN PICKLED PIGS' FEET

Serves 4 to 6

3 pounds pigs' feet, split

3½ quarts water

3½ cups red wine vinegar

2 tablespoons black peppercorns

6 bay leaves

1 tablespoon plus ¾ teaspoon salt

2 teaspoons dried thyme

1 medium carrot, peeled and diced

1 medium poblano chile, stemmed, seeded and diced

1 medium red bell pepper, cored, seeded and diced

1 medium yellow bell pepper, cored, seeded and diced

1 to 2 jalapeño chiles, stemmed, seeded and minced

½ cup olive oil

½ teaspoon freshly ground black pepper

lettuce leaves for serving

WE FIRST TASTED THIS EARTHY DISH AT A WONDERFUL CAFETERIA IN OAXACA, ONE OF OUR FAVORITE MEXICAN CITIES. THE MEAT ON PIGS' FEET, BEING SO CLOSE TO THE BONE AND WELL-EXERCISED, HAS THE MOST CONCENTRATED PORK FLAVOR. WITH THE DICED VEGETABLES, IT MAKES AN EXCEPTIONALLY CRUNCHY, COLORFUL SALAD.

Place the pigs' feet, water, 3 cups of the red wine vinegar, the black peppercorns, bay leaves, 1 tablespoon salt and the dried thyme in a large stockpot. Bring to a boil, reduce to a simmer and cook, uncovered, until the skin starts to pull away from the bones and the meat slips off easily when pierced with a fork, 1½ to 2 hours. Set aside to cool. Refrigerate 1 hour.

Remove and discard the outer layer of skin and fat from the pigs' feet and discard the bones. Slice the meat and soft cartilage into 1 × ⅛-inch-thick strips.

Place the meat, carrot and all the peppers in a large mixing bowl. Add the olive oil, the remaining ½ cup red wine vinegar, the ¾ teaspoon salt and the pepper and toss well to combine. Cover and chill 2 to 4 hours. Serve cold on lettuce-lined plates.

ANTICUCHOS (GRILLED BEEF HEART)

Serves 6

8 dried puya chiles or 4 dried California chiles, wiped clean

4 chiles de árbol

2 tablespoons annatto seeds

1 garlic clove, peeled

1 teaspoon cumin seeds

1 jalapeño chile, stemmed, seeded and roughly chopped

1/2 cup red wine vinegar

1/2 cup olive oil

2 teaspoons salt

1 pound beef hearts, trimmed of all sinew and silverskin

1 recipe Avocado Corn Relish, page 45

IN LATIN AMERICA, WHERE THEY DON'T HAVE THE LUXURY OF DISCARDING ANIMAL PARTS AS WE DO, HEARTS ARE A FAVORITE MEAT PRODUCT BECAUSE OF THEIR PURE BEEFY TASTE. EVEN IF YOU DON'T ORDINARILY EAT INNARDS, YOU OWE IT TO YOURSELF TO BRANCH OUT AND TRY THESE DELECTABLE MORSELS. WITH A ROBUST MARINADE AND SOOTHING AVOCADO CORN RELISH, THEY ARE IRRESISTIBLE. IF YOUR SKEWERS ARE BAMBOO, SOAK THEM FIRST IN WATER, THEN PLACE THEM IN THE FREEZER FOR A FEW HOURS TO PREVENT BURNING ON THE GRILL.

To make the marinade, remove the stems of the dried puyas or California and árbol chiles and shake out and discard the seeds. Place the chiles in a small saucepan and pour in enough water to cover. Bring to a boil, remove from the heat and let sit 20 minutes to soften. Drain and discard the water.

Combine the dried chiles, annatto seeds, garlic, cumin, jalapeño and red wine vinegar in a blender. Puree at high speed 1 to 2 minutes, or until thick and smooth. Add the olive oil and salt and blend again until mixed.

Cut the beef hearts into 2 × 1/4-inch strips. Place in a bowl, pour on the chile marinade and toss to coat evenly. Cover and marinate in the refrigerator at least 4 hours or overnight.

To cook, preheat the grill or broiler.

Thread 4 or 5 pieces of beef heart on each bamboo skewer. Grill the skewers until seared on all sides, 3 to 5 minutes total. Serve hot over the corn relish.

Soups, Stews

and Hearty Broths

As inveterate soup makers and eaters, we had great fun playing with some of Mexico's traditional soups like tortilla and fideo and then inventing some of our own—turkey albóndigas, corn clam chowder, puree of potatoes and poblanos, romaine lettuce soup with a Caesar salad garnish. The one Latin soup garnish we find addictive is a wedge of lime, squeezed and then tossed into the broth. Its bracing aroma hits the perfect tart note.

SOUPS WITH MEAT

TORTILLA SOUP

Serves 8

¼ cup olive oil

2 large onions, diced

4 garlic cloves, minced

3 cups Red Tomato Salsa, page 36

7 cups chicken stock or Vegetable Stock, page 115

1 dried chipotle chile, stemmed and seeded (optional)

2 teaspoons salt

¾ pound Fried Tortilla Chips, page 129

GARNISHES

1 bunch cilantro, leaves only

1 avocado, peeled, seeded and coarsely chopped

½ cup Crema, page 249, crème fraîche or sour cream

2 limes, cut into 4 wedges each

THIS EASY TORTILLA SOUP CAN BE MADE EVEN EASIER BY SUBSTITUTING STORE-BOUGHT CORN CHIPS BUT IT WON'T TASTE QUITE AS WONDERFUL. FRESHLY FRIED TORTILLAS ADD A DEFINITIVE CRISP TOASTED FLAVOR. IT MAKES A SATISFYING WEEKNIGHT SUPPER WITH A CAESAR SALAD AND SOME COLD BEER.

IF TORTILLA SOUP SITS LONG BEFORE SERVING, IT WILL THICKEN. YOU CAN SERVE IT AS IS, OR THIN WITH ADDITIONAL STOCK OR WATER. REMEMBER TO ADJUST THE SEASONINGS.

Heat the olive oil in a large stockpot or saucepan over low heat. Add the onions and cook slowly, stirring frequently, until pale brown and caramelized, 30 to 40 minutes. Add the garlic and cook 10 minutes longer.

Add the tomato salsa, chicken or vegetable stock, optional chipotle chile and salt. Bring to a boil, reduce to a simmer and cook, uncovered, 20 minutes. Stir in the fried tortilla chips and simmer 10 minutes longer, until the chips soften. Remove and discard the whole chipotle chile. Ladle into soup bowls and top each with cilantro, a few avocado chunks, a dollop of crema, crème fraîche or sour cream and a lime wedge. Serve hot.

BREAD SOUP

Serves 6 to 8

¼ cup olive oil or 4 tablespoons unsalted butter

1 onion, diced

2½ teaspoons salt

2 ripe plantains or bananas, peeled and cut into ¼-inch slices on the diagonal

5 garlic cloves, minced or pureed (see page 14)

1 bunch fresh oregano, leaves only, chopped, or ½ tablespoon dried

½ bunch fresh thyme, leaves only, chopped, or 1 teaspoon dried

small sprig of fresh rosemary, leaves only, chopped, or ¼ teaspoon dried

1½ cups canned tomatoes, diced, with the juices

6 ounces baguette (about ⅓ loaf), cut into ½-inch chunks (with crust)

6 cups chicken stock or Vegetable Stock, page 115

2 limes, cut into quarters, for garnish

OUR HEARTY SOUTH AMERICAN BREAD SOUP, BRIMMING WITH SWEET BANANAS AND FRESH HERBS, IS A GREAT WAY TO USE UP OLD BREAD. IF YOU WANT TO TRY IT AS A TRADITIONAL DRY SOUP, OR SOPA SECA, MAKE IT A DAY OR TWO IN ADVANCE AND LET THE BREAD SOAK UP THE LIQUID AS IT SITS.

Heat the olive oil or butter in a large saucepan over medium-low heat. Cook the onions with the salt until they start to caramelize, 10 to 15 minutes. Add the plantains or bananas and cook 10 minutes longer. Stir in the garlic, oregano, thyme, and rosemary and cook just until aromatic, about 3 minutes longer. Add the diced tomatoes and their juices and cook 10 minutes longer.

Add the bread chunks and chicken or vegetable stock. Bring to a boil, reduce to a simmer and cook, stirring frequently, until the bread has softened and the flavors are well blended, about 45 minutes. Ladle the soup into bowls, then squeeze a wedge of lime into each and toss in the wedge. Serve hot.

BAGUETTE

FIDEO SOUP

Serves 8

½ cup olive oil or 8 tablespoons unsalted butter

12 ounces fideo, vermicelli or angel hair pasta, broken into 1-inch pieces

3 to 4 dried or canned morita or chipotle chiles

2 pounds Roma tomatoes

8 garlic cloves, peeled

1 large onion, roughly chopped

½ cup water

2 teaspoons salt

6 cups chicken stock or Vegetable Stock, page 115

1 avocado, peeled, seeded and cut into 8 slices, for garnish

1 bunch cilantro, leaves only, chopped, for garnish

FIDEO—OR MEXICAN NOODLE SOUP—CAN BE PUT TOGETHER QUICKLY WITH PANTRY STAPLES. ALTHOUGH THE NOODLES SOFTEN AS THEY COOK IN THE BROTH, THE INITIAL TOASTING DRAMATICALLY CHANGES THEIR FLAVOR. THE BROTH TAKES ON A DEEP NUTTINESS THAT IS QUITE UNLIKE THE FLAVOR OF PASTA DISHES COOKED ANY OTHER WAY.

Heat the olive oil or butter in a large saucepan or stockpot over medium-low heat. Sauté the pasta, stirring frequently, until golden brown, being careful not to burn. Then stir in the chiles and cook 2 minutes longer.

Meanwhile, combine the tomatoes, garlic, onion, water and salt in a blender. Puree until smooth.

Add the tomato puree and chicken stock to the pot with the browned pasta. Cook over medium-low heat until the noodles soften and the flavors meld, about 15 minutes. Serve hot with the sliced avocado and cilantro as garnish.

LENTIL AND CHORIZO SOUP

Serves 12

3 to 4 dried ancho chiles, wiped clean, stemmed and seeded

1 cup water

4 thick slices bacon, cut into strips 1 inch long × $\frac{1}{8}$ inch wide

9 ounces chorizo sausage, removed from casings and crumbled

2 medium onions, diced

10 garlic cloves, minced

$2\frac{1}{2}$ cups lentils, washed and picked over

3 quarts chicken stock, Vegetable Stock, page 115, or water

2 carrots, peeled and diced

2 celery ribs, washed and diced

$1\frac{1}{2}$ teaspoons salt

$\frac{1}{2}$ teaspoon freshly ground black pepper

GARNISHES

$\frac{1}{2}$ bunch parsley, leaves only, chopped

1 bunch cilantro, leaves only, chopped

lime wedges (optional)

AS SERIOUS LENTIL LOVERS, WE ARE ALWAYS ON THE LOOK-OUT FOR NEW WAYS TO PREPARE THAT HUMBLE BEAN. IN THIS TYPICAL MEXICAN PREPARATION, THEY ABSORB THE FULL SMOKY FLAVORS OF BACON, CHORIZO AND ANCHO CHILES AND DISPEL ANY NOTIONS OF BLANDNESS. OF ALL THE CHILES, ANCHOS ARE THE SWEETEST, WITH THE MOST CONCENTRATED RIPE BELL PEPPER FLAVOR.

Toast the chiles in a dry cast-iron skillet over medium-high heat until brown all over; they will soften, bubble and release their aroma. Place the chiles in a saucepan with the water. Bring to a boil, reduce to a simmer and cook 5 minutes, or until soft. Transfer the chiles with their water to a blender or food processor and puree until smooth. Reserve.

Fry the bacon in a large heavy stockpot over medium-high heat about 4 minutes. Stir in the chorizo and sauté 3 minutes longer, or until browned. Spoon out excess fat. Add the onions and cook, stirring occasionally, until golden. Then stir in the garlic and cook for a few minutes to release its aroma. Add the lentils and reserved chile puree and sauté an additional minute.

Pour in the stock or water. Bring to a boil, reduce to a simmer and cook 10 minutes, occasionally skimming and removing the fat from the top. Stir in the carrots, celery, salt and pepper. Cook, covered, over medium-low heat about 40 minutes, skimming and discarding the fat from the top. Sprinkle with the chopped parsley and cilantro and serve hot, with the lime wedges if desired.

YUCATECAN CHICKEN AND LIME BROTH

Serves 6 to 8

2 whole chicken breasts

3 quarts chicken stock

2½ teaspoons salt

1½ teaspoons black peppercorns, cracked

1½ teaspoons dried oregano

½ head garlic, cloves separated and crushed but unpeeled

7 chicken livers (optional)

2 tablespoons chicken fat or olive oil

1 medium onion, halved and cut lengthwise into julienne

freshly ground black pepper to taste

1 small green bell pepper, cored, seeded and julienned

2 medium tomatoes, cored, seeded and julienned

juice of 2 limes

2 (1 × 3-inch) strips grapefruit zest or juice of 2 bitter limes

THIS TRADITIONAL YUCATECAN CHICKEN SOUP MAKES A WONDERFUL ONE-DISH MEAL WITH AS MUCH OR AS LITTLE GARNISH AS YOU WISH. WHATEVER YOU DO, DON'T SKIMP ON THE LIME JUICE AND ZEST THAT GIVES IT ITS TERRIFIC EDGE. SINCE FALLING IN LOVE WITH SOPA DE LIMA, WE HAVE TAKEN TO FINISHING MANY OF OUR SOUPS WITH A BRACING WEDGE OF LIME. IN THE YUCATÁN, BITTER LIME, A SMALL LIME WITH AN EXCEPTIONALLY AROMATIC SKIN, WOULD BE USED IN THIS DISH. IF YOU CAN FIND THEM, SUBSTITUTE THE JUICE OF TWO FOR THE GRAPEFRUIT ZEST.

Place the chicken breasts in a large saucepan with the chicken stock and bring to a boil. Skim and discard the foam. Add 1½ teaspoons of the salt, the black peppercorns, oregano and garlic. Reduce to a simmer and cook 30 to 35 minutes, until the meat is tender. Lift out the chicken and transfer to a platter. Cover with a damp towel and reserve.

Add, if using, the chicken livers to the stock and simmer 6 to 8 minutes. Remove with a slotted spoon and transfer to the platter with the chicken. Strain the stock through a very fine strainer, discarding the solids, and skim off any fat from the top. Reserve.

When the chicken is cool enough to handle, remove the skin and pull the meat from the bones. Shred into strips. Thinly slice the livers. Reserve.

Heat the chicken fat or olive oil in a large stockpot over medium-low heat. Cook the onions with the remaining 1 teaspoon salt and the ground black pepper until translucent, about 10 minutes. Add

GARNISHES

3 limes, cut into wedges

3 serrano chiles, stemmed, seeded if desired and minced (optional)

8 small Corn Tortillas, page 132, cut into ¼-inch strips and fried

1 avocado, peeled, seeded and cut into chunks

the green pepper and cook 5 minutes longer. Add the tomatoes, shredded chicken and livers, reserved chicken stock, lime juice and grapefruit zest or bitter lime juice. Bring to a boil, reduce to a simmer and cook until the flavors meld, 10 to 12 minutes. Remove the grapefruit zest with a slotted spoon. Serve hot with the garnishes scattered over the soup.

ROMAINE LETTUCE SOUP

Serves 6 to 8

3 tablespoons olive oil

1 large onion, sliced

1½ teaspoons salt

1 teaspoon freshly ground black pepper

2 garlic cloves, sliced

5 tomatillos, husked, washed and roughly chopped

1 to 3 jalapeño chiles, stemmed, seeded if desired

2 quarts chicken stock or water

1 large or 2 small heads romaine lettuce, cored, cleaned and roughly chopped

1 bunch cilantro, leaves and stems, chopped

1 cup plus 2 tablespoons heavy cream

2 teaspoons anchovy paste

YOU CAN SIMPLIFY THE GARNISH IN OUR MEXICAN LETTUCE SOUP BY JUST SUBSTITUTING CRÈME FRAÎCHE—BUT THEN YOU WILL MISS THE OPPORTUNITY TO TASTE AN ADAPTED CAESAR SALAD IN LIQUID FORM. ON THE OTHER HAND, THIS SOPHISTICATED LETTUCE SOUP IS STRONG ENOUGH TO STAND ALONE.

Heat the olive oil in a heavy stockpot over medium heat. Sauté the onions with the salt and pepper until translucent, 5 to 7 minutes. Add the garlic, tomatillos and jalapeño(s) and cook another 5 minutes. Pour in the chicken stock or water. Bring to a boil, reduce to a simmer and cook 20 minutes. Stir in the lettuce and cook 10 minutes longer.

Add the cilantro to the soup and bring to a boil. Remove from the heat, and puree in a blender or a food processor. If you want a more elegant soup, pass through a strainer. Bring back to a boil before serving.

Beat 1 cup of the heavy cream until soft peaks form. In a small bowl, mix the anchovy paste with the remaining 2 tablespoons cream until smooth. Fold into the whipped cream and beat a few more strokes. Serve the soup hot with dollops of the anchovy cream garnish.

CLAM AND CORN CHOWDER

Serves 6 to 8

4 tablespoons unsalted butter

1 onion, diced

1 carrot, peeled and diced

1 celery rib, washed and diced

4 ears corn, husked and kernels removed

6 baby red new potatoes, unpeeled, washed and diced

1 quart clam juice

1 cup dry white wine

3½ pounds littleneck clams, Manila clams or cockles in the shell

1 Roma tomato, cored, seeded and diced

1 red bell pepper, cored, seeded and diced

1 jalapeño chile, stemmed, seeded if desired and minced

1 bunch cilantro, leaves only, chopped

juice of 1 lime

½ teaspoon freshly ground black pepper

salt to taste

THIS SIMPLE VEGETABLE CHOWDER WITH CHUNKS OF CLAMS AND CORN KERNELS MAKES A BRIGHT AND REFRESHING SUMMER SOUP. DICED CHICKEN AND CHICKEN STOCK CAN BE SUBSTITUTED FOR THE CLAMS AND THEIR JUICE.

Melt the butter in a large stockpot over moderate heat. Sauté the onions for 10 minutes. Add the carrots, celery, corn and potatoes and sauté 2 minutes longer. Pour in the clam juice. Bring to a boil, reduce to a simmer and cook 30 minutes.

Meanwhile, bring the white wine to a boil in a large saucepan and reduce by one-third. Add the clams, cover and steam, shaking the pan occasionally, until the clams open up, 5 to 7 minutes. Remove and discard any that do not open. Remove the cover and let the clams cool in the pot. When cool enough to handle, separate the meat from the shells, reserving the juice, and chop the clams. Set aside. Reserve the cooking liquid.

Add the tomato, red pepper and jalapeño to the soup pot and cook over low heat an additional 10 minutes. Strain the reserved cooking juices and clam juice through a fine kitchen towel or coffee filter into the soup. Add the chopped clams and cook 10 more minutes. Stir in the cilantro, lime juice and pepper. Taste for salt, since the clams may be salty, and serve steaming hot.

POTATO POBLANO SOUP

Serves 6 to 8

2 strips bacon, cut into ½-inch-wide pieces

1 medium onion, chopped

4 poblano chiles, roasted, seeded, peeled (see page 11) and diced

2 teaspoons salt

1 teaspoon freshly ground black pepper

3 garlic cloves, minced

1 quart chicken stock

6 medium Yukon Gold potatoes or 8 to 10 small red new potatoes, unpeeled, chopped

1 cup Crema, page 249, crème fraîche or sour cream

½ cup grated *añejo* cheese (optional)

THIS VELVETY POTATO SOUP WITH ITS UNDERCURRENT OF CHILE HEAT WOULD BE HEAVEN WITH A GREEN SALAD AND A CRUSTY BAGUETTE ON A COLD WINTER DAY. USE THIN-SKINNED, BUTTERY YUKON GOLD POTATOES FOR THE BEST FLAVOR. THIS RECIPE WAS DEVELOPED BY BORDER GRILL CHEF CHRISTIAN SCHIRMER.

In a heavy Dutch oven or stockpot, fry the bacon over moderate heat, stirring frequently, until it starts to brown. Toss in the onions, half of the diced poblanos, the salt and pepper and cook until slightly golden, 5 to 7 minutes. Spoon out any excess fat. Stir in the garlic and cook briefly just to release the aroma, 1 to 2 minutes.

Pour in the chicken stock, add the potatoes and bring to a boil. Reduce to a simmer and cook 20 minutes. Puree in a food processor or blender just until smooth, being careful not to overprocess. Over-working will result in a gummy soup. Return to the pot, stir in the crema, crème fraîche or sour cream and bring just to a boil. Stir in the remaining poblanos for garnish. Sprinkle with grated *añejo*, if desired, and serve hot.

VEGETARIAN SOUPS

CHILLED AVOCADO AND TOMATILLO SOUP

Serves 6

6 to 8 tomatillos, husked, washed and roughly chopped

1 poblano chile, roasted, peeled and seeded (see page 11)

juice of 2 limes

1 teaspoon salt

$\frac{1}{2}$ teaspoon freshly ground black pepper

1 cup cold water plus enough ice cubes to make water rise to 2 cups in a liquid measure

2 ripe avocados, peeled and seeded

1 bunch scallions, trimmed and thinly sliced, for garnish

THIS EXCEPTIONALLY QUICK, LIGHT AVOCADO SOUP CALLS FOR ONLY TWO AVOCADOS AND NO ADDITIONAL FAT FOR SIX SERVINGS. THE TOMATILLOS GIVE IT A REFRESHING LIFT THAT MAKES IT PERFECT FOR SUMMER PICNICS AND BARBE-CUES.

Combine the tomatillos, poblano, lime juice, salt, pepper and a tablespoon or 2 of the ice water in a blender or food processor. Puree until smooth. Add the avocados with the remaining water and ice and puree briefly just to make smooth, not to incorporate air. (You do not want a frothy head.) Serve in chilled bowls with the scallions scattered on top.

SQUASH FLOWER SOUP

Serves 6 to 8

6 tablespoons unsalted butter

2 onions, sliced

1 teaspoon salt, or more to taste

½ teaspoon freshly ground black pepper, or more to taste

3 garlic cloves, sliced

2 quarts Vegetable Stock, page 115, or water

1 pound (8 cups loosely packed) zucchini or other squash flowers

2 cups half-and-half

½ cup grated *añejo* cheese

1 lime, cut into 6 or 8 wedges

SQUASH FLOWERS ARE A POPULAR INGREDIENT IN OAXACA, WHERE THEY APPEAR IN QUESADILLAS AND ELEGANT SOUPS SUCH AS THIS ONE. THE FRAGILE FLOWERS NEED ONLY BE COOKED BRIEFLY TO RELEASE THEIR INTENSE FLAVOR. WHAT A DELIGHTFULLY TASTY SOLUTION FOR SUMMER GARDENERS WITH TOO MANY POTENTIAL ZUCCHINI ON THEIR HANDS.

Melt the butter in a stockpot over moderate heat. Sauté the onions with the salt and pepper about 5 minutes. Add the garlic and cook 1 to 2 minutes longer. Pour in the vegetable stock or water. Bring to a boil, reduce to a simmer and cook 10 to 12 minutes. Then stir in the flowers and cook 5 minutes longer.

Transfer to a blender or food processor and puree until smooth. Strain back into the soup pot. Pour in the half-and-half and bring back to a boil. Season to taste with salt and pepper. Serve hot, garnished with the cheese and lime wedges.

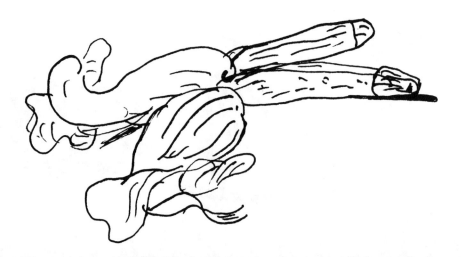

BLACK BEAN SOUP WITH CUMIN

Serves 8

2 cups dried black beans, washed and picked over

8 cups water

¼ cup olive oil or 4 tablespoons unsalted butter

2 large onions, diced

6 garlic cloves, minced or pureed (see page 14)

2 tablespoons ground cumin

1 large jalapeño chile, stemmed, seeded if desired and finely chopped

2 teaspoons salt

6 cups Vegetable Stock, page 115

1½ cups Salsa Fresca, page 40, for garnish

1 cup Crema, page 249, crème fraîche or sour cream, for garnish

THIS SIMPLE BEAN SOUP WITH ITS POTENT DOSE OF CUMIN IS A HUGE SELLER AT THE RESTAURANT. COOKING THE CUMIN BEFORE ADDING THE LIQUIDS RELEASES ITS FLAVOR AND REMOVES ANY HARSHNESS—A TECHNIQUE WE RECOMMEND WHENEVER USING DRIED SPICES.

Place the beans and water in a large saucepan over high heat and bring to a boil. Reduce the heat to low, cover and cook until the beans are soft, about 1 hour. Remove from the heat.

In another large saucepan or stockpot, heat the olive oil or butter over medium-low heat. Cook the onions until lightly browned, about 15 minutes. Then add the garlic, cumin, jalapeño and salt and cook, stirring constantly, until the garlic's aroma is released, 3 to 5 minutes. Stir in the black beans and their liquid and mix well. Pour in the vegetable stock. Turn up the heat and bring to a boil. Reduce to a simmer and cook uncovered, stirring occasionally, an additional 30 minutes.

Transfer the mixture to a blender in batches and puree until smooth, pulsing the machine on and off until it begins to liquefy. (When pureeing such a thick, hot soup be sure to leave space for air to escape so the lid doesn't blow off. We like to leave the lid slightly askew and cover with a kitchen towel to prevent accidents.)

Ladle the hot soup into bowls and garnish each serving with a generous tablespoonful of salsa fresca and crema, crème fraîche or sour cream.

WHITE BEAN SOUP
WITH TOMATOES AND HERBS

Serves 8 to 10

2 bunches fresh thyme or 1 tablespoon dried

large sprig of fresh rosemary or 1½ teaspoons dried

2 bunches fresh oregano or 1 tablespoon plus 1½ teaspoons dried

3 cups dried white beans, washed and picked over

12 cups water

¼ cup olive oil or 4 tablespoons unsalted butter

1 medium onion, diced

6 garlic cloves, minced or pureed (see page 14)

2 cups canned tomatoes, chopped, with their liquid

2½ teaspoons salt

1 teaspoon freshly ground black pepper

2 quarts Vegetable Stock, page 115, or water

2 to 2½ limes, quartered

OUR RICH TOMATO BEAN SOUP IS ENLIVENED BY LOTS OF HERBS AND A SQUEEZE OF LIME. ALWAYS COOK BEANS WITH THE COVER ON AND WITHOUT SALT TO PREVENT TOUGH SKINS AND ENCOURAGE CREAMY CENTERS.

If using fresh herbs, make an herb packet by placing a large square of cheesecloth on a counter. Place the thyme, rosemary and half of the oregano in the center, gather the ends together and tie to enclose. Remove the leaves from the remaining bunch of oregano, chop and reserve.

Combine the beans, fresh herb packet or the dried herbs and water in a large saucepan or stockpot. Bring to a boil, reduce to a simmer and cook, covered, until the beans are cooked through but still firm, 1 hour. Remove from the heat. Lift out and discard the herb bundle.

In a large stockpot, heat the olive oil or butter over medium heat. Sauté the onions until golden, 15 to 20 minutes. Stir in the garlic and cook just until the aroma is released, about 5 minutes. Add the tomatoes and their liquid, salt, pepper and half of the reserved chopped fresh oregano if using. Reduce the heat to medium-low and cook, stirring frequently, until the liquid is evaporated. Stir in the beans and their cooking liquid and cook 5 minutes longer. Pour in the vegetable stock or water. Bring to a boil, reduce to a simmer and cook about 40 minutes, or until beans are very tender.

Serve hot, garnished with the remaining fresh chopped oregano and lime wedges.

CORN AND ROASTED POBLANO SOUP

Serves 6 to 8

2 quarts milk

2 tablespoons cumin seeds

2 bay leaves

sprig of fresh rosemary or ½ teaspoon dried

¼ cup olive oil or 4 tablespoons unsalted butter

2 large onions, diced

2 teaspoons salt

4 to 6 garlic cloves, minced or pureed (see page 14)

2 teaspoons ground cumin

8 cups fresh or canned corn kernels

6 poblano chiles, roasted, peeled, seeded (see page 11) and diced

1 bunch chives, thinly sliced on the diagonal, for garnish

CORN AND ROASTED POBLANOS ARE ONE OF THOSE SWEET AND SPICY COMBINATIONS THAT GIVE MEXICAN COOKING ITS LOVELY COMPLEXITY. POBLANOS' HEAT CAN VARY WIDELY ACCORDING TO SEASON, SO REDUCE THE QUANTITY IF YOURS ARE FROM A HOT CROP. THEY ARE NOT MEANT TO OVERPOWER THE DELICATE CORN.

Combine the milk, cumin seeds, bay leaves and rosemary in a medium saucepan. Place over low heat and bring nearly to a simmer. (Do not boil.) Remove from the heat and let sit 20 minutes to infuse.

Heat the olive oil or butter in a large saucepan or stockpot over medium heat. Cook the onions with the salt until golden brown, 15 to 20 minutes. Add the garlic and ground cumin and cook, stirring frequently, 5 minutes. Then stir in the corn kernels and diced chiles and continue cooking over low heat 5 more minutes.

Using your finest strainer, strain the infused herbal milk into the corn and chile mixture. Bring to a very slow simmer over low heat. Gently simmer 15 minutes.

Pour one third of the soup into a food processor or blender and puree. Stir back into the soup pot. Serve hot with the chives as garnish.

LENTIL SOUP WITH PLANTAINS

Serves 8 to 10

2 large onions

11 garlic cloves, peeled

2 cinnamon sticks

6 whole cloves

1 bunch fresh thyme or 1 tablespoon dried

1 gallon Vegetable Stock, page 115, or water

3 cups lentils, washed and picked over

6 tablespoons olive oil or unsalted butter

2 ripe plantains or bananas, peeled, cut in half and diced

3 medium carrots, peeled, cut into quarters lengthwise and sliced into ½-inch pieces

1 tablespoon salt

¼ teaspoon ground allspice

1½ bunches cilantro, leaves and stems, chopped

LENTILS, LIKE OTHER BEANS, ARE A GOOD VEHICLE FOR THE KIND OF STRONG FLAVORINGS WE LOVE. THIS TRADITIONAL DAY OF THE DEAD SOUP—A SATISFYING MEAL IN ITSELF—IS REMINISCENT OF THE INDIAN KITCHEN WITH ITS GARLIC, FRESH HERBS AND FRAGRANT SPICES. WHEN COOKING ANY BEAN SOUP, OCCASIONALLY GIVE IT A STIR TO AVOID BURNING THE BEANS ON THE BOTTOM.

Cut 1 onion into chunks and the other into dice. Puree 6 of the garlic cloves and keep the remaining 5 whole.

Place the cinnamon sticks, whole cloves, onion chunks and whole garlic cloves in the center of a medium square of cheesecloth. Tie the ends together to form a package. Place the fresh thyme in another square of cheesecloth and tie the ends together to enclose.

Combine the vegetable stock or water and the spice and herb packages, or dried thyme, in a large saucepan or stockpot. Bring to a boil, reduce to a simmer and cook, uncovered, 30 minutes. Stir in the lentils and continue cooking until they are cooked through but still firm, 15 minutes. Strain the lentils, reserving the liquid and the thyme bundle.

Heat the olive oil or butter in a large saucepan over medium heat. Sauté the diced onion until lightly browned, about 15 minutes. Add the plantains, carrots and salt. Reduce the heat to medium-low and continue cooking until the plantains are soft and golden, 15 minutes. Stir in the pureed garlic and allspice and cook about 5 minutes longer, being careful not to scorch the garlic.

Add the lentils, their reserved liquid and the thyme bundle. Bring to a simmer and cook another 15 minutes. Remove from the heat, and remove and discard the thyme bundle. Stir in half of the chopped cilantro. Ladle into bowls and garnish with the remaining chopped cilantro.

MUSHROOM AND EPAZOTE SOUP

Serves 6 to 8

8 tablespoons (1 stick) unsalted butter

1 large onion, chopped

1 leek, white and light green parts only, washed and thinly sliced

2 medium celery ribs, washed and thinly sliced

3 garlic cloves, thinly sliced

1 pound oyster mushrooms, cleaned and finely chopped

1 1/2 teaspoons salt

1 teaspoon freshly ground black pepper

1/2 cup dry white wine

2 quarts Vegetable Stock, page 115, or water

1 tablespoon dried epazote or 2 to 3 sprigs fresh epazote (or 2 teaspoons dried oregano plus 2 to 3 sprigs fresh mint)

1 1/2 cups milk

1/2 cup sour cream

juice of 1 lime for garnish

crisply fried julienned leeks for garnish (optional)

EPAZOTE GIVES THIS SOUP A DEPTH OF FLAVOR THAT MUSH-ROOMS ALONE WON'T GIVE. THIS SMOOTHLY ELEGANT SOUP WITH ITS RICH SOUR CREAM FLAVOR IS A GOOD CHOICE FOR DINNER PARTIES, AND IT LOOKS LIKE MUCH MORE WORK THAN IT IS.

Melt the butter in a large saucepan or stockpot over medium-high heat. Sauté the onions until limp and deep golden, 12 to 15 minutes. Stir in the leek, celery, garlic and mushrooms, along with the salt and pepper. Cook, stirring frequently, until the mushrooms are golden brown, 15 to 20 minutes.

Pour in the wine and bring to a boil. Simmer until all the liquid is evaporated. Then add the vegetable stock or water and epazote (or oregano and mint). Bring to a boil, reduce to a simmer and cook about 12 minutes. Transfer to a food processor or blender and puree until smooth.

Return to the saucepan and add the milk and sour cream. Warm over medium-low heat, stirring frequently, to thoroughly heat; do not boil. Ladle into bowls and garnish with fresh lime juice and crisp fried leeks if desired.

VEGETABLE STOCK

Makes 2 ¹/₂ quarts

2 tomatoes

1 onion, peeled

1 leek, trimmed and washed

2 shallots, peeled

4 garlic cloves, peeled

2 celery ribs, washed

1 carrot, trimmed and peeled

6 corn cobs, without kernels (optional)

1 parsnip, trimmed and scrubbed
(optional)

1 fennel bulb (optional)

1 gallon water

1 small bunch parsley

1 small bunch fresh thyme or 1 teaspoon
dried

2 bay leaves

3 whole cloves

2 tablespoons cracked black pepper

2 tablespoons salt, or to taste

AFTER SPENDING YEARS AS CHEFS LOVINGLY PREPARING DE-
LICIOUS CHICKEN, VEAL AND FISH STOCKS, WE CAME SOME-
WHAT RELUCTANTLY TO VEGETABLE STOCK. NOW WE
COULDN'T DO WITHOUT ITS WHOLESOME CLEAR FLAVOR IN
OUR KITCHEN. THIS IS THE EASIEST STOCK TO PREPARE.

Roughly chop all the vegetables and place in a large pot. Pour
in the water (or enough to cover) and bring to a boil. Reduce to a
simmer, and skim and discard any impurities from the top. Add the
remaining ingredients. Simmer, uncovered, 2 hours. Strain and
store in the refrigerator up to a week or freeze.

A MEAL IN ITSELF

GREEN CHICKEN CHILAQUILES CASSEROLE

Serves 6 to 8

2 whole chicken breasts, split

salt and freshly ground black pepper

2 cups chicken stock

3½ cups Tomatillo Salsa, page 38

½ cup heavy cream

1 onion, sliced paper-thin

½ cup vegetable oil

12 day-old Corn Tortillas, page 132 (18 if individual casseroles are being made)

1 cup grated *manchego* cheese

1 cup grated *panela* cheese

½ cup grated *añejo* cheese

THESE LAYERED CHILAQUILES ARE LIKE A LASAGNE OF TORTILLAS, CHICKEN AND CHEESES, LIBERALLY MOISTENED THROUGHOUT WITH TANGY TOMATILLO SALSA. OUR CUSTOMERS GO MAD FOR THIS HOMEY DISH. IT IS A GREAT CHOICE FOR A DO-AHEAD LUNCH OR CASUAL SUPPER. FOR A MORE FORMAL PRESENTATION, SAUCE THE PLATE WITH RED TOMATO AND TOMATILLO SALSAS (PAGES 36 AND 38) AND A DOLLOP OF CREMA BENEATH THE CHILAQUILES.

Season the chicken all over with salt and pepper. Bring the chicken stock to a boil in a large saucepan. Place the breasts in the stock, reduce the heat to moderate, cover and cook until the meat is tender, about 15 minutes. Set aside to cool in the stock. When cool, remove the skin and bones and shred the meat into bite-sized pieces. Strain and reserve the stock for another use.

In a large mixing bowl, combine the fresh tomatillo salsa, heavy cream, 1 teaspoon salt, ½ teaspoon pepper, the onion and shredded chicken pieces.

Heat the vegetable oil in a medium skillet over medium-low heat. Cook the tortillas just about 5 seconds per side to soften, and then transfer to a large colander to drain.

Preheat the oven to 350°F. Butter a 4-quart casserole or 6 to 8 individual casseroles (at the restaurant, we use small soup bowls).

Combine the cheeses in a mixing bowl.

To assemble the chilaquiles, spread a thin layer of the cheese mixture over the bottom of the baking dish. Push the solids in the bowl of chicken and tomatillo sauce to the side so the liquids form a pool in the bottom. Dip all the softened tortillas in the pool to moisten. Layer one third of the moist tortillas over the cheese and top with half of the chicken mixture with its sauce. Sprinkle half of the remaining cheese over the chicken. Repeat the layers, ending with a layer of tortillas on top. Cover tightly with aluminum foil.

Bake 30 minutes or until the edges are slightly brown. Let sit for 10 minutes before slicing and serving or unmolding.

Tortilla

TURKEY ALBÓNDIGAS SOUP

Serves 6

¼ cup olive oil

8 garlic cloves, peeled

2 bunches cilantro, leaves only

1 tablespoon salt

1½ teaspoons freshly ground black pepper

1 pound ground turkey or chicken, preferably dark meat

1 large egg, beaten

⅔ cup fresh bread crumbs

⅓ cup vegetable oil

1 large leek, trimmed, washed and thinly julienned

4 medium carrots, peeled and diced

¼ head white cabbage, cored and thinly sliced

1 to 2 jalapeño chiles, stemmed, seeded and thinly julienned

3 medium Roma tomatoes, cored, seeded and diced

2½ quarts chicken stock

3 tablespoons white vinegar

WE'VE JAZZED UP ALBÓNDIGAS SOUP WITH PALE GREEN CI-LANTRO-SPIKED MEATBALLS AND A COLORFUL FRESH VEGE-TABLE BROTH. IT'S AN EXCELLENT ONE-DISH FAMILY MEAL AND IS REALLY A SNAP TO MAKE.

Combine the olive oil, garlic, cilantro and 1 teaspoon each of the salt and pepper in a blender. Puree until smooth.

In a large bowl, mix together the turkey or chicken, egg and cilantro paste. Add the bread crumbs and mix only until combined. Roll into small walnut-sized meatballs in the palms of your hands and place on a tray in the refrigerator.

Heat 2 tablespoons of the vegetable oil in a large stockpot over high heat. Sauté the leeks and carrots with the remaining 2 teaspoons salt and ½ teaspoon pepper for 2 to 4 minutes. Add the cabbage, jalapeños and tomatoes and cook, stirring frequently, until the vegetables are limp, about 3 minutes longer. Pour in the chicken stock. Bring to a boil, reduce to a simmer and cook, uncovered, 15 minutes.

Meanwhile, heat the remaining oil in a medium skillet over medium-high heat until nearly smoking. Add the chilled meatballs in batches, shaking the pan to prevent sticking, and brown on all sides. Transfer with a slotted spoon to paper towels to drain.

When all the meatballs are browned, transfer to the simmering stock and cook an additional 5 to 10 minutes. Stir in the vinegar and serve hot.

VARIATION

FOR A HEARTIER DISH, ADD A HANDFUL OR TWO OF RICE OR SMALL-SHAPED PASTA ALONG WITH THE STOCK.

RED CHICKEN CHILAQUILES STEW

Serves 4

2 cups chicken stock

1 pound skinless, boneless chicken breasts

2 tablespoons vegetable oil, plus 1 cup if using fresh tortillas

salt and freshly ground black pepper

1 onion, diced

3 garlic cloves, crushed

1 large or 2 medium tomatoes, cored, seeded and diced

2 cups Red Tomato Salsa, page 36

7 small Corn Tortillas, page 132, cut into ½-inch-wide strips, or about 2 dozen left-over chips

1 bunch cilantro, leaves only, chopped

GARNISHES

¼ cup grated *Cotija* or *añejo* cheese

½ cup diced raw onion

½ cup Crema, page 249, crème fraîche or sour cream

THIS BROTHY VERSION OF CHILAQUILES CAN BE PUT TO-GETHER IN ABOUT TWENTY MINUTES—OR EVEN LESS IF YOU HAPPEN TO HAVE LEFTOVER CHIPS AND CHICKEN IN THE HOUSE.

Bring the chicken stock to a boil in a deep skillet. Sprinkle the chicken breasts with salt and pepper and add to the broth. Cover and cook 8 to 10 minutes, or until cooked through. Then lift out the chicken, reserving the stock, wrap in a damp towel and set aside to cool.

Heat the 2 tablespoons oil in a stockpot over medium heat. Sauté the onions with 1 teaspoon salt and ½ teaspoon pepper until soft. Add the garlic and cook 2 or 3 minutes, until the aroma is released. Add the tomatoes and salsa and bring to a boil. Add the reserved chicken stock and simmer 10 minutes.

When the chicken is cool enough to handle, shred it into long strips.

If using fresh corn tortillas, pour 1 cup vegetable oil into a small deep pan and heat over medium heat. Fry the tortilla strips in batches until light brown and crisp. Drain on paper towels.

To finish, add the shredded chicken to the salsa pot and bring to a boil. Taste for salt and pepper and stir in the cilantro and fried tortilla strips or chips. Ladle into 4 bowls, sprinkle with the grated cheese and onion and top with a dollop of crema, crème fraîche or sour cream. Serve hot.

VEGETARIAN RED BEAN STEW

Serves 4 to 6

2 cups dried red beans, washed and picked over

2 quarts water

$\frac{1}{3}$ cup olive oil

1$\frac{1}{2}$ medium white onions, diced

2 teaspoons salt

$\frac{1}{2}$ teaspoon freshly ground black pepper

4 garlic cloves, crushed

2 ancho chiles, wiped clean, stemmed, seeded and lightly toasted (see page 12)

2 medium parsnips, peeled and cut into $\frac{1}{2}$-inch chunks

2 medium carrots, peeled and cut into $\frac{1}{2}$-inch chunks

2 celery ribs, peeled and cut into $\frac{1}{2}$-inch chunks

1 medium zucchini, trimmed and cut into $\frac{1}{2}$-inch chunks

1 medium yellow squash, trimmed and cut into $\frac{1}{2}$-inch chunks

Ancho Chile Salsa, page 39, for garnish

ON ONE OF OUR RESEARCH TRIPS, A MERIDA RESTAURANTEUR COOKED US AN INCREDIBLE MEAL OF RICH RED BEANS, WHICH WE TRIED TO DUPLICATE AT HOME—CALIFORNIA-STYLE. OUT WENT THE PORK PRODUCTS, WELL LOVED IN MEXICO BUT PRACTICALLY TABOO AT HOME; PLENTY OF ROOT VEGETABLES AND RICH CHILES TOOK THEIR PLACE. FOR A QUICKER GARNISH, YOU CAN SUBSTITUTE A SPOONFUL OF OLIVE OIL AND A SQUEEZE OF LIME JUICE FOR THE ANCHO CHILE SALSA, ALTHOUGH THE SALSA REALLY MAKES THE DISH SING. RED BEANS FROM EL SALVADOR HAVE THE BEST FLAVOR WE HAVE FOUND.

Place the beans and water in a saucepan and bring to a boil. Cover, reduce to a simmer and cook until the small beans are creamy, not powdery, 45 to 60 minutes. Remove from the heat.

Heat the olive oil in a large stockpot or Dutch oven over medium heat. Cook the onions with 1 teaspoon of the salt and the black pepper until golden, 10 to 15 minutes. Add the garlic, reduce the heat and cook, stirring frequently, until the aroma is released.

Pour the red beans with their liquid into the stockpot, along with the toasted anchos, parsnips and carrots. Turn the heat up to medium and cook at a low boil for 10 minutes. Add the remaining vegetables and 1 teaspoon salt. Simmer until all the vegetables are soft, about 15 minutes longer. Remove and discard any chile skin that floats to the top. Ladle into large bowls and serve hot with a dollop of ancho salsa.

POZOLE WITH TOMATILLOS

Serves 8 to 10

2 tablespoons lard, vegetable oil or chicken fat

2 medium onions, diced

4 to 6 garlic cloves, minced

6 cups chicken stock

2 cups canned hominy, drained

4 cups Carnitas, page 136

4 cups Tomatillo Salsa, page 38

salt and freshly ground black pepper to taste

GARNISHES

10 radishes, trimmed and thinly sliced

½ red onion, finely diced

¼ head cabbage, shredded

2 limes, cut into wedges

LIKE MANY TRADITIONAL MEXICAN FOODS, POZOLE HAS NU-MEROUS VARIATIONS. THE ONE COMMON INGREDIENT, HOWEVER, IS HOMINY, KERNELS OF DRIED WHITE FIELD CORN TREATED WITH LIME. OUR CARNITAS AND GREEN SALSA VERSION IS A ZESTY, MEATY ONE THAT WOULD MAKE A WONDERFUL ONE-DISH MEAL FOR A BUFFET—SAY ON NEW YEAR'S DAY.

Melt the fat in a large saucepan over medium-high heat. Sauté the onions until golden brown and limp, about 10 minutes. Then add the garlic and cook briefly, just until the aroma is released.

Add the chicken stock, hominy and carnitas, reduce the heat and simmer, uncovered, about 10 minutes. Add the tomatillo salsa and bring to a boil. Reduce to a simmer and cook an additional 5 minutes. Season to taste with salt and pepper. Ladle into bowls and serve with the garnishes for sprinkling at the table.

TONGUE STEW

Serves 3 to 4

1 pound veal tongue

3 quarts water

1 small white onion, quartered

1 carrot, peeled and cut into 4 pieces

1 celery rib, cut into 4 pieces

4 bay leaves

1 whole clove

1½ teaspoons salt

2 teaspoons black peppercorns

2 tablespoons unsalted butter

1 medium red onion, diced

6 garlic cloves, minced

2 medium or 5 Roma tomatoes, cored, seeded and diced

2 jalapeño chiles, stemmed, seeded if desired and diced

½ bunch oregano, leaves only, chopped

IN THIS REFINED STEW, WE ELEVATE TONGUE, A POPULAR MEXICAN MEAT, BY COOKING IT JUST ENOUGH AND THEN FINISHING IT QUICKLY WITH OTHER ASSERTIVE INGREDIENTS LIKE JALAPEÑOS AND OREGANO. EVEN THOSE WHO DON'T ORDINARILY EAT TONGUE WILL LOVE THIS DISH ONCE THEY GET BEYOND ANY PRECONCEIVED NOTIONS.

Place the tongue in a medium saucepan with the water, or enough to cover. Add the white onion, carrot, celery, bay leaves, clove, salt and black peppercorns. Bring to a boil, reduce to a simmer and cook, uncovered, 1½ to 2 hours, until tender. Transfer the tongue to a cutting board, cover with a damp towel and set aside to cool. Strain and reserve the stock.

Peel and discard the tongue's skin. Cut the meat into 3 × ½-inch julienne strips.

Melt the butter in a large saucepan over medium-high heat. Sauté the red onion until well browned, about 10 minutes. Stir in the garlic and sauté an additional 2 minutes. Add the tomatoes and jalapeños and sauté 2 minutes longer. Then add the tongue and reserved stock. Simmer 8 minutes. Sprinkle in the oregano, and remove from the heat. Serve over white rice.

VARIATION

FOR TONGUE TACOS, FOLLOW THE RECIPE THROUGH THE ADDITION OF THE BOILED TONGUE TO THE SKILLET. DO NOT ADD THE STOCK AND COOK JUST TO HEAT THROUGH. SERVE ON SMALL CORN TORTILLAS (PAGE 132), ALLOWING 2 PER PERSON, WITH THE SAME GARNISHES AS FOR CARNITAS TACOS (SEE PAGE 136).

SEAFOOD STEW

Serves 4

3 Roma tomatoes

5 garlic cloves, peeled

1 tablespoon olive oil

1 1/2 onions, julienned

1 teaspoon salt

1/2 teaspoon freshly ground black pepper

1/2 cup dry white wine

1 quart fish stock

2 carrots, peeled, cut in half lengthwise and then into 1/8-inch slices

3 small boiling potatoes, peeled, cut in half lengthwise and then into 1/8-inch slices

1 morita chile, stemmed, seeded and julienned

1 1/2 pounds assorted fish fillets, such as flounder, sea bass and snapper, cut into 2-inch chunks

1/2 cup chopped cilantro leaves for garnish

lime wedges for garnish

USE WHATEVER SEAFOOD IS FRESH AT THE MARKET FOR THIS UNCOMPLICATED STEW. ROASTING THE TOMATOES AND GARLIC GIVES THE BROTH AN EXTRA DASH OF MEXICAN FLAVOR.

Preheat the broiler. Place the tomatoes and garlic on a baking tray and broil until the tomatoes are charred all over and garlic is golden. (Tuck the garlic under the tomatoes as necessary to prevent burning.) Transfer to a blender and puree.

Heat the olive oil in a heavy soup pot over moderate heat. Cook the onions with the salt and pepper until translucent. Pour in the wine, turn the heat up to high and reduce by half. Pour in the fish stock and bring back to a boil. Add the carrots, potatoes, garlic-tomato puree and morita chile and cook 3 to 5 minutes. Add the fish. Cook 2 to 3 minutes, until the fish is just done. Sprinkle in the cilantro and serve immediately with lime wedges.

OREGANO-BRAISED LAMB SHANKS

Serves 6

6 lamb shanks (about 1 pound each)

2 tablespoons ground cumin

1 tablespoon salt

2 teaspoons freshly ground black pepper

flour for dredging

¾ cup vegetable oil

2 onions, cut into 8 wedges each

3 carrots, peeled and cut into 2-inch lengths

1 head garlic, cloves separated, peeled and halved lengthwise

2 bunches oregano, stems and leaves separated, leaves chopped

2 cups dry white wine

2 tablespoons tomato paste

2½ quarts chicken stock

5 bay leaves

3 medium tomatoes, cored, seeded and diced

6 ounces *añejo* cheese, grated (1½ cups)

WE LIKE TO SERVE PEASANT DISHES LIKE THESE TENDERLY BRAISED LAMB SHANKS IN BIG BOWLS TO HOLD THE DELICIOUS, RICH BROTH—PERFECT FOR DIPPING BREAD OR TORTILLAS. THIS IS A GREAT CHOICE WHEN YOU NEED TO COOK A SPECIAL DINNER IN ADVANCE.

Preheat the oven to 350°F.

Wash the lamb and pat dry. Sprinkle the shanks all over with the cumin, salt and pepper. Roll the shanks in flour to coat well and pat off any excess.

Heat the oil in a large Dutch oven over medium-high heat until almost smoking. Cook the shanks, in batches if necessary, until golden brown all over, about 10 minutes. Remove and reserve. In the same oil, sauté the onions and carrots until they begin to brown, about 6 minutes. Add the garlic and sauté about 4 minutes longer. Remove with a slotted spoon, and then carefully pour off all the fat.

Place the shanks back in the pan. Cover with the browned vegetables and the oregano stems and pour in the wine. Bring to a boil over high heat and reduce the liquid by half. Stir in the tomato paste, chicken stock and bay leaves, cover and bring to a boil.

Transfer to the oven and bake 1½ hours, or until tender. A fork plunged into the thickest part should slide out easily. Remove from the oven, lift out the meat and keep warm. Lift out the vegetables and discard.

Skim and discard the fat from the stock in the pan. Bring to a boil over high heat. Stir in the tomatoes and oregano leaves and remove from the heat. To serve, in each soup bowl place a lamb shank. Top with the hot broth and sprinkle with the cheese.

TACO

Tortillas, Tacos, Tortas and Burritos

Since we first started traveling to Mexico, we have been in love with the fresh, simple, satisfying snacks found in the marketplaces and at fast food stands. At the Border Grill we have tried to recapture that spirit with the freshest corn tortillas and a wide variety of carefully prepared, liberally garnished soft tacos made to order. We serve the traditional stewed meats, roasted chicken and grilled beef you expect to see on tacos, as well as a few surprises: potatoes and roasted peppers, adobo-soaked lamb, duck confit with chipotle salsa, poached seafood sprinkled with a small garden of chopped vegetables. If you're feeling ambitious, make all the fixings and invite a crowd over to make their own tacos.

This kind of casual food welcomes improvisation. Each of the fillings could be garnished with nothing more complicated than a slice of avocado, some chopped onion and cilantro or a squeeze of lime and still be thoroughly enjoyable. Likewise, feel free to use leftover meats and perk them up with our suggested salsas and garnishes.

BREAD AND TORTILLAS

FRIED TORTILLA CHIPS

**Serves 4 to 6 as an appetizer
with dips**

vegetable oil for deep-frying

12 large Corn Tortillas, page 132, cut into
6 wedges each

½ teaspoon salt

OUR HOMEMADE CORN TORTILLAS ARE GREAT FOR CHIP MAKING SINCE THERE IS LESS MOISTURE TO FRY OUT THAN IN STORE-BOUGHT VARIETIES. THE KEY TO MAKING CHIPS AT HOME IS TO START WITH STALE DRY TORTILLAS.

Pour the oil into a large pot, to a depth of 2 to 3 inches, and heat to 375°F. Test by dropping in a piece of tortilla. If it bubbles immediately and rises to the surface, the oil is ready.

Fry the wedges a handful at a time, stirring to separate, until very lightly browned, 1 to 2 minutes. Remove with a strainer or slotted spoon, shaking off excess oil, and transfer to paper towels to drain. Sprinkle with salt while still warm, and continue frying in batches.

BOLILLOS

**Makes 9 (6-inch) rolls or
1 (14-inch) loaf**

1 cup warm water

1 tablespoon dry yeast

½ teaspoon sugar

1 cup lukewarm milk

3¼ cups bread flour

3¼ cups plus 1 tablespoon all-purpose flour

2 tablespoons salt

1½ teaspoons baking powder

vegetable oil for coating

2 tablespoons unsalted butter, softened

THESE SLIGHTLY SOUR, CRUSTY WHITE ROLLS ARE EATEN FOR BREAKFAST OR USED TO MAKE SANDWICHES IN MEXICO. YOU OWE IT TO YOURSELF TO TRY THIS RECIPE—IT IS ONE OF OUR ABSOLUTE FAVORITE BREADS. AS AN ADDED BONUS, THE BREAD OR ROLLS FREEZE VERY WELL.

To make the sponge, in a large mixing bowl or bowl of an electric mixer with a paddle, combine the water, yeast and sugar and stir or mix to dissolve the yeast. Add the milk, ¾ cups each of the bread flour and all-purpose flour and mix until smooth. Set aside at room temperature for 30 minutes.

Mix together the remaining 2½ cups bread flour and 2½ cups of the all-purpose flour in another bowl. Scoop out 1 cup of this mixture and transfer to a small bowl. Add 1 tablespoon of the salt and the baking powder and toss with a fork to combine. Add this flour mixture to the yeast sponge and stir or mix to combine.

Continue mixing, gradually adding enough of the remaining flour mixture so that the dough leaves the sides of the bowl. Change to the dough hook or remove from the bowl and knead, gradually adding more flour, until the dough is not tacky, but moderately firm and dry. Continue kneading 10 to 15 minutes longer. Transfer the dough to a lightly oiled bowl and turn to coat all sides. Cover with a damp towel and set aside to rise in a warm spot until doubled in bulk, about 1 hour.

Punch down the dough and briefly knead on a lightly floured surface. Divide the dough into 9 portions for rolls or leave whole for a 14-inch loaf. Roll each portion into a ball or shape into a loaf and set aside to rest 10 minutes.

In a small bowl, knead together the softened butter and remaining 1 tablespoon all-purpose flour. Pull each of the balls into a 6-inch-long log. With a knife, make a shallow slit down the center of each and spread some of the butter mixture inside. Enclose by briefly rolling on the counter by hand and then transfer, face down, to a baking sheet to rise 30 to 45 minutes. Follow the same procedure if making a loaf. The rising is complete when a finger pressed in the dough leaves a mark.

Preheat the oven to 425°F.

Combine the remaining 1 tablespoon salt and 1 cup water in a spray bottle. Generously spray the rolls or loaf all over. Line a baking tray with parchment paper, transfer the dough to it and spray the top and sides again. Bake 5 minutes and then turn the oven temperature down to 325°F. Bake rolls an additional 10 minutes, a loaf an additional 20 minutes, until golden brown and hollow-sounding when rapped on the bottom. Be careful not to overbake.

Bread

CORN TORTILLAS

Makes 24 small taco-size tortillas or 12 large quesadilla-size tortillas

4 cups finely ground deep yellow masa harina

2¾ cups cold water

1 teaspoon salt

CAKEY FRESH CORN TORTILLAS BEAR ABOUT AS MUCH RE-SEMBLANCE TO THE STORE-BOUGHT VARIETY AS A ROUGH-HEWN COUNTRY LOAF DOES TO WONDER BREAD. WE ENJOY TORTILLAS MADE FROM A DEEP YELLOW MASA HARINA BE-CAUSE IT HAS A MORE INTERESTING, VERY STRONG CORN FLAVOR. THERE REALLY ISN'T MUCH TECHNIQUE INVOLVED IN MAKING THESE NUBBLY LITTLE TORTILLAS FROM SCRATCH AND THEY ADD IMMEASURABLY TO ANY FOODS THEY ARE SERVED WITH. IN TACOS, THEY PROVIDE THE CORN FLAVOR THAT IS INTEGRAL TO THE DISH.

Combine the masa harina, water and salt in a large mixing bowl and stir until smooth. The dough should be slightly sticky and form a ball when pressed together. To test, flatten a small ball of dough between your palms. If the edges crack, add water to the dough, a tablespoon at a time, until a test piece does not crack.

Divide the dough into 24 golf ball–size pieces for tacos or 12 large balls for quesadillas. Place on a platter and cover with a damp towel.

Line a tortilla press with 2 sheets of plastic cut from a plastic freezer bag or other heavy duty plastic bag.

Heat a dry cast-iron skillet, nonstick pan or comal until moderately hot. Flatten each ball of dough in the tortilla press, then remove the plastic from the top and, holding the tortilla with your fingertips, peel off the bottom sheet. Lay the tortillas one by one on the skillet and cook about 30 to 45 seconds per side, pressing the top of each tortilla with your fingertips to make it puff.

Place the hot tortillas on a towel. When they are still warm but not hot, stack and wrap in a towel. Serve immediately or let cool, wrap well in plastic or a plastic bag and store in the refrigerator up to a week.

MASa

FLOUR TORTILLAS

Makes 8 large tortillas

2½ cups all-purpose flour

scant ½ cup vegetable shortening (3½ ounces)

1 teaspoon salt

1 cup warm water

FLOUR TORTILLAS DEMAND A BIT MORE TIME AND TECHNIQUE THAN CORN SINCE YOU HAVE TO MAKE A DOUGH. ON THE OTHER HAND, THE DOUGH CAN BE MADE IN ADVANCE AND KEPT IN THE REFRIGERATOR UNTIL IT IS TIME TO GRIDDLE. SINCE THEY DO NOT HAVE AS MUCH FLAVOR AND CHARACTER AS CORN, WE TEND TO THINK OF FLOUR TORTILLAS AS A SIMPLER BREAD TO SERVE WITH FOODS LIKE SQUID SAUTÉ (PAGE 183) OR OUR POZOLE (PAGE 121). ONCE AGAIN, THE DIFFERENCE BETWEEN THESE AND STORE-BOUGHT MAKES THEM WELL WORTH THE EFFORT.

Place the flour, shortening and salt in the bowl of a heavy-duty mixer. Beat with the paddle until crumbly, 3 to 5 minutes. With the mixer running, gradually add the warm water and continue mixing until the dough is smooth, about 3 minutes.

Divide the dough into 8 pieces. Roll each into a ball and place on a baking tray or board. Cover with a towel and let rest at room temperature at least 15 minutes or up to 1 hour.

Cut out eight 12-inch squares of waxed or parchment paper for stacking the tortillas. On a lightly floured board, roll each ball into a 10-inch circle, and transfer to a paper square. Stack on a baking tray or platter and refrigerate until cooking time. Uncooked tortillas can be kept in the refrigerator, well wrapped with paper squares between the layers, up to 2 days.

To cook, heat a dry griddle or 12-inch skillet (Teflon is great) over medium heat. Carefully peel off the paper and cook the tortillas, one at a time, until puffy and slightly brown, 30 to 45 seconds per side. Set aside to cool slightly on a towel-lined platter. Bring to the table wrapped in a towel for warmth, or wrap well and refrigerate or freeze for quesadillas or other dishes.

TACOS

Carnitas Tacos

**Makes 12 tacos
(about 3 cups carnitas)**

2 pounds lard

2½ pounds pork butt, trimmed and cut into 2-inch cubes

2 teaspoons salt

½ teaspoon freshly ground black pepper

1 cup Chile de Árbol Salsa, page 35

MELTINGLY SOFT CARNITAS, OR STEWED PORK, CAN BE SERVED AS A TRADITIONAL ENTRÉE WITH PICKLED RED ONIONS (PAGE 46) OR WRAPPED IN CORN TORTILLAS AS A TACO. DON'T LET THE LARD IN THE RECIPE SCARE YOU. ALL THE FAT IS RENDERED *OUT* OF THE MEAT BY LONG SLOW COOKING, SO WHEN YOU LIFT OUT THE TENDER PORK MEAT, THE FAT STAYS BEHIND.

Melt the lard in a large deep saucepan over moderate heat. Add the pork, salt and pepper, and simmer until tender, being careful not to crisp the meat, about 1 hour and 10 minutes. Remove the pork with a slotted spoon and set aside to cool. (Reserve the lard for future use.)

When cool enough to handle, shred the meat by hand or with the tines of a fork. Remove and discard any remaining fat. Transfer to a medium saucepan, add the árbol salsa and cook over moderate heat, stirring frequently, 5 to 8 minutes.

Carnitas can be kept in the refrigerator up to 5 days and reheated before assembling the tacos.

For carnitas tacos, dip 24 small Corn Tortillas (page 132) in water, shaking off excess. Toast one at a time in a nonstick pan over moderate heat about 1 minute per side. Wrap in a towel to keep warm. For each taco, stack 2 tortillas and layer with warm carnitas, Salsa Fresca (page 40), chopped cilantro and avocado slices or simply chopped onion and cilantro.

CARNE ASADA TACOS

Makes 12 tacos

1 1/2 pounds skirt, flank or tri-tip steak

2 tablespoons olive oil

1 teaspoon salt

1/2 teaspoon freshly ground black pepper

WE LIKE OUR CARNE ASADA, OR GRILLED STEAK, TACOS TOPPED BY A CRUNCHY SALAD OF CABBAGE, SCALLIONS AND RADISHES. THESE ARE ALSO A WONDERFUL WAY TO USE LEFT-OVER STEAK, AND THE SALSA CRUDA THAT MAKES THESE TACOS SPECIAL IS A SNAP TO MAKE.

Slice the beef across the grain into 1/4-inch slices. Combine in a mixing bowl with the oil, salt and pepper. Toss well to coat.

Heat the grill or heat a dry cast-iron skillet until smoking. Sear the meat until light pink in the center, about 30 seconds per side. Transfer to a cutting board. Cut into 1/2-inch-wide strips and reserve in a bowl with the juices.

For carne asada tacos, toast 24 small Corn Tortillas (page 132) as for Carnitas Tacos (see page 136), and keep warm. For each taco, stack 2 tortillas and layer with carne asada strips. Top with about a tablespoon of Pureed Tomato Salsa Cruda (page 38). Garnish with shredded white cabbage, scallions, thinly sliced radishes and avocado slices.

POTATO AND RAJAS TACOS

Makes 12 tacos

3 medium boiling potatoes, peeled and cut into ½-inch dice

4 cups Creamy Rajas, page 62

THESE VEGETARIAN TACOS, WITH THEIR EARTHY COMBINATION OF CORN MASA, POTATOES AND PEPPERS, MAKE A DEEPLY SATISFYING SMALL MEAL.

Bring a medium saucepan of salted water to a boil and cook the potatoes until just tender, being careful not to overcook, 6 to 8 minutes. Drain, pat dry and spread in a single layer on a tray to cool.

When ready to serve, heat the rajas in a medium saucepan over medium-low heat, stirring frequently, just to heat through. Add the potatoes and stir occasionally until heated through.

For potato and rajas tacos, toast 24 small Corn Tortillas (page 132) as for Carnitas Tacos (see page 136) and keep warm. For each taco, stack 2 tortillas and layer with the potato rajas mixture. Top with Salsa Fresca (page 40) and an avocado slice and serve.

CHICKEN TACOS

Makes 12 tacos

1½ pounds marinated chicken legs, roasted and shredded (see page 195)

THIS IS OUR EASIEST, BEST-SELLING AND MOST VERSATILE TACO. IF YOU WANT TO USE LEFTOVER CHICKEN MEAT YOU CAN REHEAT IT WITH ANY ONE OF OUR SALSAS, SUCH AS ROASTED TOMATO (PAGE 37), RED TOMATO (PAGE 36) OR ÁRBOL (PAGE 35) AND YOU ARE SURE TO COME UP WITH A CROWD-PLEASING MEAL.

Toast 24 small Corn Tortillas (page 132) as for Carnitas Tacos (see page 136). For each taco, stack 2 tortillas. Divide the chicken and place on tortillas. Top with Salsa Fresca (page 40), sliced avocado and chopped cilantro.

BLACK BEAN AND CHEESE TACOS

Makes 12 tacos

1½ cups Refried Black Beans, page 53

1 cup grated cheese mix (see page 9)

Preheat the oven to 350°F.

Toast 24 small Corn Tortillas (page 132) as for Carnitas Tacos (see page 136). Make 12 stacks of 2 tortillas each on a baking sheet. Spread with the beans and grated cheese mix and bake 6 to 8 minutes to melt the cheese and heat through. Remove and top with Salsa Fresca (page 40), an avocado slice and chopped cilantro.

LAMB ADOBADO TACOS

Makes 12 tacos

2½ pounds lamb shoulder, trimmed and cut into 2-inch cubes

2 teaspoons salt

½ teaspoon freshly ground black pepper

2 cups Adobo, page 42

4 poblano chiles

½ cup grated *manchego* cheese

¼ cup grated *panela* cheese

¼ cup grated *añejo* cheese

CHUNKS OF FLAVORFUL LAMB SHOULDER BAKED IN SWEET-AND-SOUR ADOBO SAUCE CAN BE MADE IN ADVANCE AND EVEN FROZEN. THIS IS AN EXCEPTIONALLY RICH, SATISFYING TACO—A GOOD CHOICE FOR A WEEKEND LUNCH, WITH A WATERCRESS AND JICAMA SALAD (PAGE 169).

Preheat the oven to 350°F.

Season the lamb all over with the salt and pepper and place in a single layer in a roasting pan. Pour on the adobo sauce and toss to coat. Bake, uncovered, 45 minutes, then cover and bake 45 to 60 minutes longer, until the meat is soft and flaky.

Transfer the meat to a cutting board. Pour the pan juices into a bowl or measuring cup and skim and discard the fat. Shred the meat. The lamb and pan juices may be kept together in the refrigerator up to 5 days. Warm over moderate heat 5 to 7 minutes before assembling the tacos.

For lamb adobado tacos, preheat the oven to 350°F.

Roast, peel (see page 11), seed and slice the poblano chiles. Mix together the grated cheeses. Toast 24 small Corn Tortillas (page 132) as for Carnitas Tacos (see page 136) and keep warm.

Make 12 stacks of 2 tortillas each on a baking sheet. Divide the lamb evenly among the tortillas. Top with poblano strips, sprinkle evenly with the cheeses and bake 3 to 4 minutes, to melt the cheese and heat through. Serve immediately.

SEAFOOD TACOS

Makes 12 tacos

6 leaves green leaf lettuce, washed and halved

2 pounds cooked lobster or crabmeat, shrimp or salmon (preferably poached)

1½ cups Citrus Cucumber Relish, page 44

½ avocado, peeled, seeded and mashed

1 cup fresh or frozen sweet peas, blanched

½ bunch red radishes, washed, trimmed and thinly sliced

½ bunch cilantro, leaves only, roughly chopped

2 limes, halved

¼ cup extra-virgin olive oil

OUR FISH TACOS ARE OVERFLOWING WITH BITS AND PIECES OF BRIGHT, FRESH VEGETABLES AS WELL AS CHUNKS OF MOIST, JUST-COOKED FISH. THEY DEMAND PLENTY OF NAPKINS, IF NOT A BIB, FOR FULL ENJOYMENT. WE CAN THINK OF NO BETTER USE FOR LEFTOVER GRILLED OR POACHED FISH THAN THESE SUPERB, LIGHT TACOS—THE PERFECT SUMMER PARTY FOOD.

Toast 12 small Corn Tortillas (page 132) as for Carnitas Tacos (see page 136). Lay the tortillas out on a counter. Line each tortilla with a piece of lettuce and spread the fish on top. Cover with 2 tablespoons of cucumber relish, a dab of avocado, a tablespoon of sweet peas, a few slices of radish and a pinch of cilantro. Finish each with a squeeze of lime juice, a teaspoon of juice from the relish and a teaspoon of olive oil. (When you lift these tacos, they should be spilling with juice.) Serve immediately.

VERY IMPORTANT NO CHOLESTEROL

DUCK TACOS

Makes 12 tacos

1 roasted duck (cooked as on page 207)

1 tablespoon duck fat, chicken fat or vegetable oil

1 onion, thinly sliced

1 teaspoon salt

½ teaspoon freshly ground black pepper

2 red bell peppers, roasted, peeled, seeded (see page 11) and julienned

1 cup Chipotle Salsa, page 34, plus extra for garnish

1 tablespoon honey

freshly squeezed lime juice

1 avocado, peeled, seeded and sliced

THESE ARE OUR LEAST TRADITIONAL, MOST IMPRESSIVE, SPECIAL-OCCASION TACOS. AS WITH THE CARNITAS AND LAMB TACOS, SLOW COOKING PRODUCES THE MOST FLAVORFUL AND TENDER MEAT—REALLY ESSENTIAL FOR A GREAT TACO.

Remove the duck meat from the bones, discarding all skin and sinew. Shred the meat.

Heat the fat in a medium skillet over medium-high heat. Sauté the onion with the salt and pepper until translucent. Add the red peppers and duck meat and cook, stirring frequently, until heated through. Keep warm.

Combine the salsa, honey and a squeeze of fresh lime juice.

For tacos, toast 12 small Corn Tortillas (page 132) as for Carnitas Tacos (see page 136). Divide the filling and center on each tortilla. Top each with a tablespoon of salsa and a slice of avocado, and serve.

TORTAS

THE MEXICAN FAST-FOOD REPERTOIRE ALSO INCLUDES DELICIOUS OVER-STUFFED SANDWICHES CALLED TORTAS. USUALLY SERVED ON THE CRUSTY WHITE ROLLS CALLED BOLILLOS, TORTAS CAN BE FILLED WITH WHATEVER LEFTOVER MEATS, FRESH CHEESES, PEPPERS, SALSAS AND BEANS ARE ON HAND, BUT HERE ARE A FEW OPTIMAL COMBINATIONS TO GET YOU STARTED. IF BOLILLOS ARE UNAVAILABLE (AND YOU DON'T FEEL LIKE BAK-ING), FRENCH OR SOURDOUGH ROLLS CAN BE SUBSTITUTED. OUR ONLY OTHER ADVICE IS TO MAKE SURE TO SPREAD ALL THE FILLINGS OUT TO THE EDGES OF THE BREAD SO EACH BITE IS AS DELICIOUS AND MESSY AS THE CENTER.

TURKEY TORTA

Makes 1 sandwich

unsalted butter

1 Bolillo, page 130, cut in half lengthwise

¼ cup Refried Black Beans, page 53, or good-quality canned refried beans

2 teaspoons Cracked Black Pepper Garnish, page 43

1 4-ounce slice raw turkey breast, pounded to an ⅛-inch thickness

salt and freshly ground black pepper to taste

olive oil

¼ cup Pickled Red Onions, page 46

IT IS AMAZING HOW THE PICKLED ONIONS TURN THIS TUR-KEY SANDWICH INTO SOMETHING VERY SPECIAL. IF YOU HAVE LEFTOVER TURKEY, SKIP THE SEARING STEP AND GENTLY REHEAT THE MEAT.

Preheat the oven to 300°F.

Preheat the grill or broiler. Lightly butter both cut sides of the bolillo. Toast on the hot grill or under the broiler. Spread the bottom half with the black beans and warm in the oven. Sprinkle the black pepper garnish on the top half.

Season the turkey all over with salt and pepper. Lightly coat a skillet with olive oil and place over high heat. Cook the turkey about 30 seconds per side. Place the turkey on the bread spread with the pepper garnish. Top the bread spread with the beans with the red onions. Place on the turkey, cut in half and serve.

BARBECUE CHICKEN TORTA

Makes 1 sandwich

1 tablespoon vegetable oil

¼ onion, julienned

¼ teaspoon salt

¼ teaspoon freshly ground black pepper

½ poblano chile, roasted, peeled, seeded (see page 11) and julienned

¼ cup Adobo, page 42

½ cup shredded or chopped cooked chicken

1 Bolillo, page 130

1 tablespoon mayonnaise

1 lettuce leaf

2 tomato slices

THIS PEPPER AND ADOBO MIXTURE WORKS WELL WITH JUST ABOUT ANYTHING, SO DON'T HESITATE TO USE IT TO DRESS UP LEFTOVER STEAK OR OTHER MEATS.

Heat the oil in a small skillet over medium-high heat. Sauté the onion with the salt and pepper until translucent. Add the poblano, adobado and chicken, stir well and cook just to heat through.

Split open the bolillo. Spread the inside with the mayonnaise. Line one side with the lettuce leaf and the other with the tomato slices. Spoon in the warm chicken mix, press together and serve.

Vegetarian Torta

Makes 1 sandwich

1 Bolillo, page 130, cut in half lengthwise

unsalted butter

1 tablespoon mayonnaise

½ cup Refried Black Beans, page 53, or good-quality canned refried beans

½ cup grated *manchego* cheese

½ poblano chile, roasted, peeled, seeded (see page 11) and julienned

½ red bell pepper, roasted, peeled, seeded (see page 11) and julienned

4 green olives, pitted and sliced

¼ avocado, peeled, seeded and sliced

½ tomato, thinly sliced

1 large radish, trimmed and thinly sliced

lettuce leaves

WE LOVE THE CHALLENGE OF CREATING INTENSELY DELICIOUS VEGETARIAN DISHES SUCH AS THIS SANDWICH, WHICH WAS CHOSEN AS ONE OF THE YEAR'S BEST BY THE *LOS ANGELES TIMES*. PEOPLE MAY UNDERESTIMATE THE SOPHISTICATION OF SUCH A DISH BUT TO US, AS CHEFS, SIMPLICITY IS WHERE THE TRUE TEST LIES.

Preheat the broiler. Generously butter both cut sides of the bolillo. Toast under the broiler. Coat both sides with mayonnaise. Spread the beans over the bottom half and sprinkle with the cheese. Place under the broiler just to melt the cheese. Then top with the roasted pepper strips, olives, avocado, tomato, radishes and lettuce. Cover with the top piece of bread.

cheese

BURRITOS

CHICKEN BURRITOS

Serves 4

4 Flour Tortillas, page 134

1 cup Refried Black Beans, page 53, or good-quality canned refried beans, warmed

2 cups shredded roasted chicken (see page 195) or leftover cooked chicken meat

2 tablespoons Crema, page 249, crème fraîche or sour cream

1 avocado, peeled and sliced

2 large tomatoes, sliced

2 small bunches watercress, trimmed, washed and dried

2 tablespoons freshly squeezed lime juice

2 tablespoons olive oil

½ teaspoon salt

½ teaspoon freshly ground black pepper

THIS LIGHTENED BURRITO TASTES LIKE A SALAD WRAPPED UP IN A DELICIOUS FLOUR TORTILLA.

Spread the tortillas on a counter. Spread each with a strip of warm black beans down the center. Top with the chicken (warmed), crema, crème fraîche or sour cream, avocado and tomatoes. Lightly toss the watercress with the lime juice, olive oil, salt and pepper and place over each burrito. Fold the bottom quarter of each tortilla up and then roll from the side into a cylinder.

VEGETARIAN BURRITOS

Serves 4

2 zucchini, trimmed and sliced lengthwise into wedges

2 yellow squash, trimmed and sliced lengthwise into wedges

2 red bell peppers, cored, seeded and cut into quarters

¼ cup olive oil

2 tablespoons minced garlic

1 bunch oregano, leaves only, chopped

1 teaspoon salt

1 teaspoon freshly ground black pepper

4 Flour Tortillas, page 134

1 cup Avocado Corn Relish, page 45

½ cup Tomatillo Salsa, page 38

HERE IS A BURRITO MINUS THE TRADITIONAL BEANS BUT FULL OF GREAT STRONG FLAVORS AND ZESTY SEASONING.

Toss the vegetables in a large bowl with the oil, garlic, oregano, salt and pepper. Let sit at least 1 hour to marinate.

Preheat the grill.

Grill the vegetables over hot coals (or cook in a hot dry skillet) until tender, turning occasionally to avoid charring.

To assemble, warm the tortillas briefly on the grill to render them pliable, and spread them out on a counter. Divide the vegetables and place in a strip down the center of each tortilla. Top with the avocado corn relish and drizzle with some of the tomatillo salsa (being careful not to oversauce, or the burritos will be soggy). Fold the bottom quarter of each tortilla up and then roll from the side into a cylinder. Serve immediately, with the remaining salsa on the side.

VARIATION

IN PLACE OF THE GRILLED VEGETABLES, SMEAR EACH TORTILLA WITH ½ CUP WARMED REFRIED BLACK BEANS (PAGE 53) AND SPRINKLE WITH CHEESE. TOP WITH ½ RECIPE WATERCRESS AND JÍCAMA SALAD (PAGE 169). THEN ADD THE AVOCADO CORN RELISH AND ROLL UP AS DIRECTED.

Morning Foods

DON'T LET THE EGG DISHES IN THIS CHAPTER FOOL YOU. THOUGH THEY ARE GROUPED TOGETHER AS MORNING FARE, THESE HEARTY DISHES WOULD TASTE TERRIFIC ANY TIME OF THE DAY OR NIGHT. IF YOU HAVE NEVER TASTED A MEXICAN-STYLE BREAKFAST, YOU ARE IN FOR A TREAT. WITH THEIR CHILES AND GENEROUS SAUCES THEY ARE TRULY EYE-OPENERS.

POACHED EGGS IN CHILE BROTH

Serves 6

2 medium tomatoes, roasted (see page 12)

4 cups chicken stock

2 tablespoons olive oil

1 medium onion, julienned

1 1/2 teaspoons salt

1 1/2 teaspoons freshly ground black pepper

2 garlic cloves, minced

2 red bell peppers, roasted, seeded, peeled (see page 11) and julienned

2 poblano chiles, roasted, seeded, peeled (see page 11) and julienned

6 large eggs

1/2 cup grated *añejo* cheese, for garnish

1/2 cup sour cream, for garnish

warm Flour Tortillas, page 134, for serving

THE KEY TO THIS TYPICAL MEXICAN BREAKFAST IS TO THOR-
OUGHLY CHAR THE TOMATOES AND CHILES THAT ARE THE
FOUNDATION FOR THE DELICIOUS BROTH. THIS DISH IS AS
COMFORTING AS CAN BE.

Place the unpeeled roasted tomatoes in a blender with 1 cup of the chicken stock. Puree until smooth and reserve.

Heat the olive oil in a large skillet over medium-high heat. Sauté the onions with the salt and pepper until golden brown, 10 to 12 minutes. Add the garlic and cook 1 minute longer. Add the julienned red peppers and poblanos, roasted tomato puree and the remaining 3 cups chicken stock. Bring to a boil, reduce to a simmer and cook 5 minutes to marry the flavors.

To poach the eggs, crack one at a time into a cup and gently slide into the simmering broth. Cook 4 to 6 minutes, basting the tops occasionally with hot broth.

With a slotted spoon, gently lift out the eggs and place one in each soup bowl. Ladle the broth over and garnish with the grated cheese and a dollop of sour cream. Serve immediately with warm flour tortillas.

DRUNKEN EGGS

Serves 6

6 ounces slab bacon (skin optional)

1 large yellow onion, diced

1 teaspoon salt

½ teaspoon freshly ground black pepper

3½ cups chicken stock

2 medium tomatoes or 4 small Roma tomatoes, cored, seeded and diced

4 large eggs, beaten

½ cup grated *añejo* cheese

2 to 4 serrano chiles, stemmed and chopped (seeds optional)

warm Corn Tortillas, page 132, for serving

THESE SPICY, MESSED UP LOOKING DRUNKEN EGGS ARE SWIMMING IN A SMOKY MIX OF CHICKEN SOUP AND BACON, GARNISHED WITH CRISP FRESH SERRANO CHILES. SERVE WITH PLENTY OF TORTILLAS OR, EVEN BETTER, THE DELICIOUS MEXICAN BEAN TOAST CALLED MOLLETTE. FOR MOLLETTE, SPLIT BOLILLOS OR CHUNKS OF FRENCH BREAD IN HALF AND LIGHTLY GRILL. THEN SMEAR WITH A LAYER OF REFRIED BLACK BEANS, SPRINKLE WITH CHEESE AND HEAT IN THE OVEN.

Remove the bacon skin, if any, and reserve if desired. Cut the bacon into ¼-inch cubes. Fry over low heat until all the fat is rendered. Drain on paper towels. Reserve 2 tablespoons of the fat.

Heat the reserved bacon fat in a stockpot over medium-low heat. Cook the onions with the salt and pepper until deep brown, 10 to 15 minutes. Add the chicken stock and bacon skin, if using, simmer 15 minutes. Remove the bacon skin. Skim and discard the fat from the top, and bring the broth to a boil. Stir in the fried bacon and tomatoes and return to a boil.

Gently stir in the beaten eggs just until cooked and thready, 1 to 2 minutes, being careful not to overblend. Remove from the heat. Ladle into warm bowls and sprinkle with the cheese and serrano chiles. Serve immediately with warm corn tortillas.

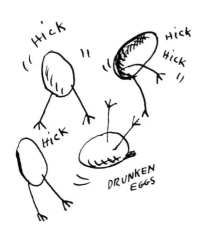

HUARACHES WITH EGGS

Serves 6

1 recipe masa for Corn Tortillas, page 132

1 1/2 cups Refried Black Beans, page 53, or good-quality canned refried beans

1/2 cup vegetable oil

3 tablespoons unsalted butter

12 large eggs

1 1/2 cups Red Tomato Salsa, page 36

1 1/2 cups Tomatillo Salsa, page 38

1 cup sour cream

HUARACHES, TWICE-COOKED MASA TURNOVERS STUFFED WITH BLACK BEANS, ARE COLORFUL, EXUBERANT, TASTY AND ECONOMICAL. SINCE WE FIRST TASTED THEM AT FIVE O'CLOCK ONE MORNING AT A MEXICO CITY PRODUCE MARKET, WHERE THEY WERE SOLD AS STREET FOOD, THEY HAVE BEEN ONE OF OUR FAVORITES.

Divide the masa into 12 balls. Press each between 2 sheets of plastic wrap to form 6-inch-long ovals about 1/16 inch thick. On one side of each, smear 2 tablespoons refried black beans. Fold over the masa to enclose the filling and seal the edges by pressing. Then flatten, between plastic sheets again, by patting between the palms of your hands until the shape resembles the sole of a shoe, or *huarache.* They may be stacked between sheets of plastic or waxed paper and stored in a plastic bag in the refrigerator up to 2 days.

Heat a dry nonstick pan or well-seasoned griddle over medium heat. Toast the huaraches, turning frequently, 2 to 3 minutes per side or until speckled and golden on the outside and puffy.

Then heat the vegetable oil in another skillet over medium-high heat. Fry the huaraches about 30 seconds per side, until slightly brown but not crisp. Drain on paper towels and keep warm in a 200°F oven.

Melt the butter in a large nonstick skillet over moderate heat. Fry the eggs, sunny-side up, just until set, about 1 minute.

To serve, place 2 huaraches on each plate. Top one with red salsa and one with green. Top each with an egg and spoon a dollop of sour cream in the center where the two salsas meet. Serve hot.

RAJAS AND EGGS SCRAMBLE

Serves 2

1 small new potato, such as Yukon Gold, peeled and cut into 1/2-inch dice

4 large eggs

1/2 teaspoon salt

1/2 teaspoon freshly ground black pepper

1 tablespoon unsalted butter

3/4 cup Creamy Rajas, page 62

1/2 cup grated *añejo* cheese

THE CREAM IN THE RAJAS KEEPS THESE EGGS EXCEPTIONALLY LOOSE AND MOIST. THE RAJAS CAN BE MADE IN ADVANCE SO ALL THAT IS LEFT TO DO IN THE MORNING IS TO SCRAMBLE THE EGGS.

Bring a small saucepan of salted water to a boil. Add the potatoes and cook just until tender, 6 to 8 minutes. Drain, pat dry and set aside to cool.

In a small bowl, beat the eggs with the salt and pepper.

Melt the butter in a large nonstick skillet over moderate heat. Sauté the potatoes, stirring and tossing frequently, until they are cooked through and just begin to brown, 10 to 12 minutes. Stir in the rajas and cook until hot and bubbly. Pour in the eggs. Cook, stirring constantly, until the eggs are just set. (This is a moist, soft dish.) Sprinkle with the grated cheese and serve immediately.

GUAVA EMPANADAS

Serves 6

8 ounces cream cheese, softened

4 ounces *Cotija*, Monterey Jack or *manchego* cheese, grated

1 cup guava paste

2 teaspoons freshly squeezed lime juice

½ cup sugar

1 teaspoon ground cinnamon

1 recipe Pie Dough, page 257

1 large egg, beaten, for egg wash

SERVE THESE GENEROUS PASTRIES OF MELTED CHEESE AND GUAVA JAM WITH CARAFES OF CAFE CON LECHE AND MEXICAN CHOCOLATE FOR THE ULTIMATE SOOTHING WEEKEND BREAKFAST. ANY OTHER TART JAM, SUCH AS PLUM, CAN BE SUBSTITUTED FOR THE GUAVA, WHICH IS AVAILABLE IN LATIN MARKETS.

Mix together the cream cheese and grated cheese. Stir together the guava paste and lime juice. Combine the sugar with the cinnamon. Set the three mixtures aside.

On a lightly floured board, roll the dough out to a rectangle about 16 × 11 inches and ⅛ inch thick. With the tip of a sharp paring knife, cut out six 5-inch circles, using a pot lid as a guide. Remove the dough scraps. Spread the cheese over half of each circle and then top with the guava, leaving a ½-inch border along the edge. Brush the edges with some of the beaten egg and then fold the dough over to enclose the filling. Seal the edges by pressing the top to bottom with the tines of a fork. Chill at least 30 minutes before baking.

Preheat the oven to 350°F.

Place the empanadas on a baking sheet and brush the tops with the egg wash. Sprinkle with the cinnamon sugar. With a sharp knife, cut three small slits in the top of each for steam to escape. Bake 30 minutes, or until the dough is golden. Transfer to a cooling rack to cool slightly. Serve warm.

HUEVOQUILES

Serves 4

1 cup Red Tomato Salsa, page 36

1 cup heavy cream

4 cups Fried Tortilla Chips, page 129 (left-over chips are fine)

½ cup grated cheese mix (see page 9)

1 tablespoon unsalted butter

4 large eggs

1 tablespoon plus 1 teaspoon sour cream

THIS RICH, MOIST TAKE ON CHILAQUILES REMINDS US OF A CREAMY, SAVORY BREAKFAST CEREAL. TOPPED WITH FRIED EGGS, IT IS ESSENTIAL COMFORT FOOD.

Combine the salsa and cream in a saucepan and bring to a boil. Add the corn chips, reduce the heat and simmer, stirring frequently, until the chips soften, about 15 minutes. Stir in the grated cheese and remove from the heat.

Melt the butter in a large nonstick skillet. Fry the eggs, sunny-side up, just until set. Ladle the corn chip mixture into bowls. Top each with a fried egg and 1 teaspoon of sour cream. Serve immediately.

BANANA PANCAKES WITH COCONUT SYRUP

Serves 4 to 6

1 ½ cups all-purpose flour

1 tablespoon sugar

½ teaspoon salt

1 teaspoon baking soda

1 teaspoon baking powder

1 large egg

1 cup buttermilk

¼ cup whole milk

1 tablespoon melted unsalted butter

about 3 tablespoons unsalted butter

3 ripe bananas, cut into ⅓-inch slices

Coconut Syrup, recipe follows, warmed

THESE FLUFFY BUTTERMILK PANCAKES, OUR BEST-SELLING ITEM AT SUNDAY BRUNCH, ARE EVEN BETTER IF YOU LET THE BATTER SIT IN THE REFRIGERATOR OVERNIGHT. SLICED STRAWBERRIES OR THAWED FROZEN BLUEBERRIES CAN BE SUBSTITUTED FOR THE BANANAS, AND PURE MAPLE SYRUP WOULD ALSO BE DELICIOUS.

Sift together the flour, sugar, salt, baking soda and baking powder.

In a large bowl, whisk together the egg, buttermilk, milk and melted butter. Add the dry ingredients. Stir until the flour disappears, being careful not to overbeat the batter.

Preheat the oven to 200°F.

Melt ½ tablespoon of the butter in a large cast-iron skillet over medium heat. Ladle about ¼ cup of batter into the pan for each pancake. Immediately press 4 or 5 banana slices into each, so the batter oozes slightly over the fruit. Cook until bubbles appear and then flip and cook on the other side, about 3 minutes total. Transfer the pancakes to a platter and keep warm in the oven while you cook the remaining batches, adding butter to the pan as needed. Serve hot with warm coconut syrup.

COCONUT SYRUP

Makes 2 cups

1 (14.5-ounce) can unsweetened coconut milk

1 cup sweetened shredded coconut

¾ cup packed brown sugar

Combine all the ingredients in a small heavy saucepan. Bring to a boil, reduce to a simmer and cook 20 minutes, stirring occasionally. Transfer to a blender and puree until smooth. Serve immediately. Coconut syrup can be stored in the refrigerator 2 weeks and reheated.

watercress

Jícama

Salads

Though we couldn't find much of a salad tradition in Mexico, salads are the most important part of the menu here in Los Angeles. To blend the cultures, we took native Mexican ingredients like watercress, cucumber and amaranth and combined them in the kind of dishes that satisfy our health as well as taste concerns. Most make terrific main courses, especially in the summertime when a little mound of well-dressed greens can elegantly take the place of a cooked sauce under fish, chicken or beef.

TURKEY TOSTADA SALAD

Serves 4 as an entrée,
8 as an appetizer

1 pound thinly sliced raw turkey breast, pounded between sheets of plastic to a thickness of 1/8 inch.

salt and freshly ground black pepper

1 medium red onion, diced

1 bunch cilantro, leaves only, chopped

8 to 10 romaine lettuce leaves, cut into a thin chiffonade

1 medium tomato, cored, seeded and diced

3/4 cup grated *añejo* cheese

2/3 cup red wine vinegar

1 cup olive oil

2 teaspoons salt

2 teaspoons freshly ground black pepper

8 large Corn Tortillas, page 132

oil for frying

1 cup Refried Black Beans, page 53, or good-quality canned refried beans

3 tablespoons Crema, page 249, crème fraîche or sour cream

1 large or 2 medium avocadoes, peeled, seeded and thinly sliced

THIS LIGHT, CRUNCHY TURKEY SALAD SERVED ON A CRISP TORTILLA IS MUCH CLOSER IN CONCEPT TO THE TOSTADAS FOUND IN MEXICO THAN THE HUGE CHEESE-LADEN CONCOCTIONS SERVED IN MANY MEXICAN-AMERICAN RESTAURANTS. THEY MAKE A WONDERFUL, EASY FAMILY MEAL THAT CAN BE PUT TOGETHER AT THE LAST MOMENT. YOU CAN FRY THE TORTILLAS IN ADVANCE OR EVEN PURCHASE SHELLS IN THE SUPERMARKET, SEAR THE TURKEY UP TO A DAY IN ADVANCE AND CUT UP THE VEGETABLES AHEAD OF TIME.

Preheat the grill or broiler, or heat a cast-iron skillet over high heat and thinly coat with oil. Season the turkey all over with salt and pepper. Cook the slices 1 minute per side. Set aside to cool.

Cut the turkey into 1/2-inch squares and place in a bowl with the red onion and cilantro.

In another bowl, combine the shredded lettuce, tomato and half the cheese. Combine the red wine vinegar, olive oil, and 2 teaspoons each salt and pepper in a small jar. Cover and shake vigorously to combine.

Pour oil to a depth of 1/2 inch in a small pan for frying. Fry the tortillas on both sides until crisp and drain on paper towels.

Meanwhile, heat the beans through in a small pot.

To assemble, spread a thin layer of beans on each crisp tortilla. Top with about 1 teaspoon crema, crème fraîche or sour cream and a few avocado slices. Pour enough dressing on the reserved turkey mixture to coat generously and toss well. Divide among the tortillas. Toss the remaining dressing with the salad and generously cover each tostada with salad. Sprinkle with the remaining cheese.

BRISKET SALAD

Serves 4

1 bunch scallions, white and light green parts, thinly sliced on the diagonal

6 radishes, trimmed and thinly sliced

1 red bell pepper, cored, seeded and julienned

1 green bell pepper, cored, seeded and julienned

1/4 head white cabbage, finely shredded

1/2 cup olive oil

1/2 cup chipotle vinegar (from Pickled Chipotles, page 46) or red wine vinegar

1 teaspoon sugar

1 teaspoon salt

1/2 teaspoon freshly ground black pepper

2 garlic cloves, minced or pureed (see page 14)

1 to 3 Pickled Chipotles, page 46, or chipotles canned in adobo, stemmed, seeded and roughly chopped

6 lettuce leaves

1 pound beef brisket, cooked (see page 214) and thinly sliced across the grain

1 avocado, peeled, seeded and thinly sliced, for garnish

FEEL FREE TO USE LEFTOVER BRISKET—OR ANY OTHER CUT OF BEEF YOU MAY HAVE ON HAND—FOR THIS CASUAL, FULL-BODIED SALAD. THE KEY TO THE SPECIAL DRESSING IS CHIPOTLE CHILES, WHICH PAIR SUBLIMELY WITH BEEF.

In a large bowl, combine the scallions, radishes, red and green bell peppers and cabbage. Add the olive oil, vinegar, sugar, salt, black pepper, garlic and chipotle chile(s). Toss well to combine and coat the vegetables.

Line 6 serving plates with the lettuce leaves. Fan the brisket slices over the lettuce. Top each with a mound of dressed vegetables and drizzle any dressing remaining in the bottom of the bowl over the brisket. Garnish with the avocado slices and serve with crusty bread.

TOMATO SALAD WITH FIELD GREENS

Serves 6

4 bunches bitter greens, such as dandelion, amaranth, escarole, chard, spinach or watercress

2 to 3 teaspoons salt

2/3 cup extra virgin olive oil

juice of 2 lemons

1 teaspoon salt

3/4 teaspoon freshly ground black pepper

2 large or 3 medium ripe tomatoes, cored

1 large chunk (about 8 ounces) aged Parmesan cheese

CHILLED BLANCHED GREENS ON COOL RIPE TOMATO SLICES MAKE A GREAT SUMMER SALAD, OR STARTER FOR A CASUAL SUPPER. WE PARTICULARLY LIKE AMARANTH, ALSO KNOWN AS JOSEPH'S COAT, FOR THIS SIMPLE HEALTHFUL DISH.

Wash the greens well and trim and discard any tough stems.

Bring a very large pot of water to a boil and add 2 to 3 teaspoons salt. (A large quantity of water is the key to avoiding bitterness.) Have ready a large bowl of iced water. Add the greens to the rapidly boiling water and cook 2 to 3 minutes, until tender but not mushy. Drain in a colander, shaking off excess water and then plunge the hot greens into the iced water. When the greens are cool, remove any ice from the surface and drain in a colander again. Then squeeze out any excess water and place in a bowl in the refrigerator.

Mix together the olive oil, lemon juice, salt and pepper. Toss with the cooked greens to coat thoroughly. Return to the refrigerator.

Cut the tomatoes into 1/2- to 3/4-inch slices. Arrange on 6 salad plates or a platter. Top the tomatoes with the cold dressed greens and garnish with shavings of Parmesan cheese. Serve cold or at room temperature.

SHAKE SALAD

Serves 4 to 6

1 medium jícama (about ¾ pound)

2 oranges

¼ small pineapple

1 very small red onion, thinly sliced

¼ to ½ dried habanero chile, stemmed, seeded and finely chopped to a powder, or cayenne pepper to taste

juice of 1 lime

1 teaspoon salt

WE LOVE THE TROPICAL COMBINATION OF FRUIT AND SALT FOUND IN THIS SPICY FAT-FREE SALAD. IT IS JUST THE RIGHT KIND OF BRIGHT, CRUNCHY FOOD TO REAWAKEN DULLED SENSES. IN MEXICO, IN FACT, IT IS A TRADITIONAL HANG-OVER CURE.

Peel the jícama, including the fibrous layer just beneath the skin. Thinly slice the flesh and then cut into thin 1-inch strips. Place in a bowl.

Working over a bowl to catch the juices, peel the oranges and cut between the membranes to remove the sections. Remove the seeds. Transfer the orange sections and juice to the bowl with jícama.

Peel and core the pineapple, and trim out any eyes, being careful to save the juice. Cut the pineapple into 1 × ⅛-inch strips and add to the jícama bowl along with the juice.

Add the red onion, habanero chile or cayenne pepper, lime juice and salt. Toss well and chill for 30 minutes. Serve cold.

BABY GREENS WITH ALMOND VINAIGRETTE

Serves 6

18 asparagus spears (about 1 pound), hard ends trimmed

1 tablespoon olive oil

$1/2$ pound oyster or white mushrooms, stems and caps finely sliced

1 garlic clove, minced

2 tablespoons chopped fresh parsley

juice of 1 lemon

$1/4$ teaspoon salt

$1/4$ teaspoon freshly ground black pepper

1 pound (6 cups loosely packed) baby greens, such as oak leaf, mâche and watercress

Almond Vinaigrette, recipe follows

DISTINCTIVE SALAD DRESSINGS SUCH AS THIS ONE ARE SO EASY TO MAKE IT IS A PITY TO DRESS YOUR EVENING GREENS WITH ANYTHING LESS. FEEL FREE TO SUBSTITUTE LEFTOVER STEAMED VEGETABLES LIKE BROCCOLI OR GREEN BEANS FOR THE ASPARAGUS GARNISH.

Blanch the asparagus in a large saucepan of boiling salted water until bright green, about 1 to 2 minutes. Immediately transfer to a bowl of iced water. Drain and cut on the diagonal into 2-inch-long pieces. Set aside.

Heat the olive oil in a medium skillet over medium heat until smoking. Sauté the mushrooms just to soften, about 1 minute. Add the garlic and sauté briefly until the aroma is released. Remove from the heat. Stir in the parsley, lemon juice, salt and pepper and set aside to cool.

In a large mixing bowl, lightly toss the baby greens with about half of the almond vinaigrette. Divide into 6 portions and place on serving plates. Divide the mushrooms and sprinkle across the top.

In the same bowl, toss the blanched asparagus with the remaining vinaigrette. Divide among the salads, fanning the spears across the top.

ALMOND VINAIGRETTE

Makes ³/₄ cup

¹/₂ cup slivered blanched almonds

¹/₄ cup olive oil

2 tablespoons freshly squeezed lime juice

2 tablespoons water

¹/₂ teaspoon salt

¹/₄ teaspoon freshly ground black pepper

Preheat the oven to 350°F.

Spread the almonds on a baking sheet and bake until slightly golden, about 5 minutes. Set aside to cool.

When the almonds are cool, transfer to a blender along with the remaining dressing ingredients. Puree until smooth. Store in a container in the refrigerator up to 5 days.

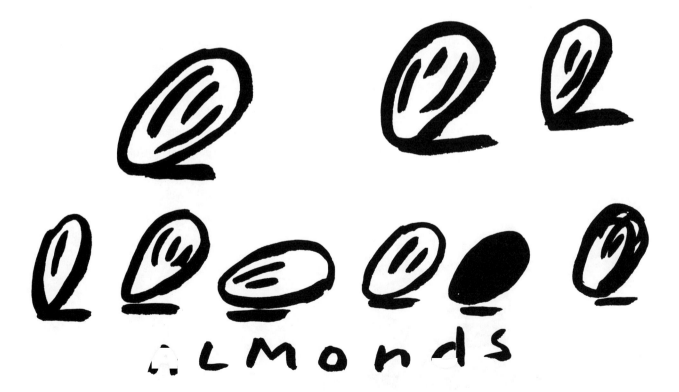

SEARED TUNA SALAD WITH TOMATO EPAZOTE COMPOTE

Serves 4

1 to 1¼ pounds tuna, about 1 inch thick

1 teaspoon salt

2 tablespoons minced or pureed garlic (see page 14)

¼ cup cracked black pepper

⅓ cup olive oil

½ pound mixed baby lettuces

¼ cup Lime Olive Oil Dressing, page 169

1 avocado, peeled, seeded and sliced

Tomato Epazote Compote, recipe follows

Cracked Black Pepper Garnish, page 43

THIS STRONGLY FLAVORED MAIN COURSE SALAD IS AN EASY DISH FOR ENTERTAINING SINCE THE COMPOTE, GREENS AND DRESSING ALL CAN BE MADE IN ADVANCE—ONLY THE FISH NEEDS LAST-MINUTE COOKING. THEN THE WHOLE THING CAN BE PUT TOGETHER IN FIVE MINUTES OR LESS.

Cut the tuna into 4 long narrow rectangular pieces. Sprinkle with the salt and then coat with the pureed garlic. Roll in the cracked pepper to coat evenly.

Heat a large skillet over high heat and add the oil. Sauté the tuna, shaking the pan frequently to avoid sticking, about 30 seconds each on all four long sides. Transfer to a cutting board and set aside to cool slightly.

Meanwhile, toss the baby lettuces with the dressing. Divide and arrange on one side of each of 4 serving plates. Place one-quarter of the tomato compote opposite each salad. Cut each piece of tuna into 8 to 10 slices and fan out over the compote. Arrange the avocado slices over the salad, drizzle with cracked pepper garnish and serve.

TOMATO EPAZOTE COMPOTE

Makes 1 ¹/₂ cups

3 tablespoons olive oil

1 small red onion, thinly sliced

6 Roma tomatoes, cored, seeded and diced

1 tablespoon capers

1 garlic clove, minced

8 large epazote leaves or ¹/₄ cup fresh oregano leaves, chopped

2 tablespoons red wine vinegar

1 teaspoon salt

¹/₄ teaspoon cracked black pepper

Heat 1 tablespoon of the olive oil in a small skillet over medium-high heat. Sauté the red onion until wilted, about 5 minutes. Set aside to cool.

Combine the remaining 2 tablespoons oil and all the remaining ingredients in a bowl. Add the cooled onion, toss well and set aside.

CUCUMBER AND BREAD SALAD

Serves 4 to 6

1½ Bolillos, page 130, or ¼ loaf crusty Italian bread

6 pickling cucumbers, peeled and cut into ¾-inch chunks

1 small red onion, thinly sliced

3 Roma tomatoes, chopped

½ cup green olives, pitted and cut in half

6 ounces *panela* cheese, cut into ½-inch cubes

¼ cup red wine vinegar

¼ cup olive oil

½ bunch cilantro, leaves only, chopped

¾ teaspoon salt

½ teaspoon cracked black pepper

lettuce leaves for serving

THIS HEARTY BREAD SALAD CONTAINS JUST THE SORT OF IN-GREDIENTS WE ARE LIKELY TO KEEP ON HAND FOR QUICK FAMILY MEALS.

Cut the bread, with crusts, into ½-inch cubes. Spread on a tray to thoroughly dry, 1 to 2 hours, or dry in a 250°F oven for 30 to 45 minutes.

Mix the cucumbers, onion, tomatoes, olives and cheese together in a bowl. Add the remaining ingredients and the bread cubes. Toss well, cover and chill 30 minutes. Serve cold on lettuce-lined plates.

WATERCRESS AND JÍCAMA SALAD

Serves 6

1 medium jícama, peeled

4 bunches watercress, trimmed and washed

LIME OLIVE OIL DRESSING

½ cup olive oil

2 tablespoons freshly squeezed lime juice

¼ teaspoon salt

⅛ teaspoon freshly ground black pepper

WATERCRESS, ONE OF OUR FAVORITE GREENS, IS FOUND EVERYWHERE IN MEXICO, WHERE ITS TART BITE STRIKES A RE-FRESHING BALANCE WITH SPICY FOODS. IT CAN BE LESS EX-PENSIVE THAN OTHER BITTER GREENS AND WE LIKE THE FACT THAT THE STEMS ARE TENDER ENOUGH TO EAT.

Thinly slice the jícama and then cut into ⅛-inch-wide strips. Combine the jícama and watercress in a bowl.

Whisk together the olive oil, lime juice, salt and pepper. Pour over the salad and toss well to coat. Serve immediately on chilled plates.

VARIATION

FOR A FULLER-BODIED SALAD, FAN AVOCADO SLICES ACROSS THE TOP AND DRIZZLE WITH CRACKED BLACK PEPPER GARNISH (PAGE 43).

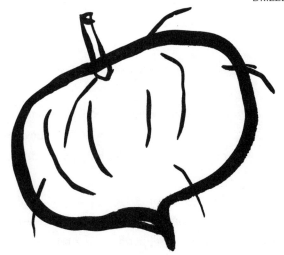

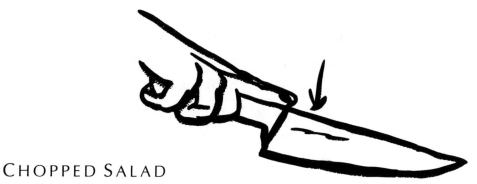

CHOPPED SALAD

**Serves 6 as an entrée,
8 as an appetizer**

2 medium carrots, peeled

¾ pound small boiling potatoes

½ pound white mushrooms

1 medium zucchini, ends trimmed

1 medium yellow squash, ends trimmed

1 small jícama, peeled

15 radishes, trimmed

4 Roma tomatoes, cored and seeded

¾ cup plus 3 tablespoons olive oil

1¾ teaspoons salt

¾ teaspoon freshly ground black pepper

1½ bunches oregano, leaves only

⅔ cup red wine vinegar

2 jalapeño chiles, stemmed, seeded and roughly chopped

RATHER THAN JUST CHOPPING A BUNCH OF VEGETABLES AND TOSSING THEM TOGETHER, WE PRESENT EACH ONE IN THE BEST POSSIBLE LIGHT IN THIS POPULAR SALAD. WE BLANCH THE TOUGH ONES TO SOFTEN THEM, BRIEFLY SAUTÉ THE SOFT ONES TO BRING OUT THEIR FLAVORS AND LEAVE THE CRUNCHY ONES ALONE TO PRESERVE THEIR FRESHNESS. THIS IS A GOOD SALAD FOR A PICNIC OR POTLUCK SINCE IT KEEPS WELL.

Cut the carrots, potatoes, mushrooms, squashes, jícama, radishes and tomatoes into ½-inch dice.

Bring a large saucepan of salted water to a boil. Blanch the carrots and potatoes for 3 minutes. Drain and immediately plunge into iced water to stop the cooking. When cool, drain thoroughly, pat dry with paper towels and reserve.

Heat a large skillet over high heat. Then add 3 tablespoons of the olive oil. Sauté the mushrooms and squashes with ½ teaspoon of the salt and ¼ teaspoon of the pepper for 2 to 3 minutes. Then spread out on a cookie sheet to cool.

1 red bell pepper, cored, seeded and roughly chopped

1 medium poblano chile, stemmed, seeded and roughly chopped

1 cup grated *Cotija* or *añejo* cheese

6 to 8 large lettuce leaves

1 large avocado, peeled, seeded and thinly sliced

Cracked Black Pepper Garnish, page 43

In a large mixing bowl, combine the sautéed squashes and mushrooms, blanched potatoes and carrots, jícama, radishes and tomatoes.

Make the dressing: In a blender, combine two-thirds of the oregano leaves, the remaining ¾ cup olive oil, the red wine vinegar, remaining 1¼ teaspoons salt and ½ teaspoon pepper, and the chopped peppers and puree. Pour the dressing over the vegetables, add the grated cheese and toss. Cover and chill 20 to 30 minutes.

To serve, line plates with lettuce leaves. Pile on the salad, arrange the avocado slices on top and drizzle with cracked pepper garnish. Sprinkle with the remaining fresh oregano and serve.

SPINACH SALAD WITH CREAMY YOGURT DRESSING

Serves 6

2 red bell peppers, roasted, seeded, peeled (see page 11) and julienned

1 bunch oregano, leaves only, roughly chopped

½ cup green olives, pitted and roughly chopped

2 tablespoons olive oil

½ teaspoon salt

¼ teaspoon freshly ground black pepper

1 bunch spinach, stems removed, washed and dried

¼ red cabbage, cored and finely shredded

3 Roma tomatoes, cored, seeded and julienned

1 small red onion, julienned

1 small jícama, peeled and julienned

2 pickling cucumbers, peeled and julienned

Creamy Yogurt Dressing, recipe follows

OUR YOGURT DRESSING IS LIGHT AND ACIDIC, WITH JUST A HINT OF GARLIC TO MAKE IT SING. THIS CREAMY SALAD WOULD ALSO BE GREAT AS A BASE UNDER FISH.

BEAR IN MIND THAT THE VEGETABLES LISTED HERE, AS IN MOST OF OUR SALAD RECIPES, ARE MEANT TO BE SUGGESTIONS. OTHER VEGETABLES, ESPECIALLY THE ONES AVAILABLE IN YOUR REFRIGERATOR RIGHT NOW, CAN EASILY BE SUBSTITUTED. JUST LOOK FOR SIMILAR TEXTURES AND TASTES TO THOSE WE CALL FOR. YOU CAN ALSO ELIMINATE A STEP BY JUST TOSSING THE ROASTED PEPPER STRIPS AND OLIVES WITH THE SPINACH RATHER THAN MARINATING THEM FOR A GARNISH.

Mix together the red pepper strips, oregano, olives, olive oil, salt and pepper in a small bowl and reserve.

For the salad, tear the spinach leaves into bite-sized pieces. Place in a large bowl with the cabbage, tomatoes, red onion, jícama and cucumbers and toss well. Refrigerate until ready to serve.

CREAMY YOGURT DRESSING

Makes about 1 cup

juice of 1 lemon

2 tablespoons olive oil

1 teaspoon salt

½ teaspoon freshly ground black pepper

1 to 2 garlic cloves, roughly chopped

1 cup plain yogurt (as pure as possible, without stabilizers, perctin, etc.)

For the dressing, combine the lemon juice, olive oil, salt, pepper and garlic in a blender and puree until smooth. Add the yogurt and blend briefly to combine.

To serve, pour the yogurt dressing over the salad and toss to coat evenly. Divide and place on 6 serving plates. Top each with a large spoonful of the red pepper garnish.

SPICY CABBAGE SLAW

Serves 6 to 8

1 white cabbage, finely sliced

2 carrots, peeled and shredded

2 teaspoons celery salt

½ to 1 teaspoon red pepper flakes

1 tablespoon dried Mexican oregano, crushed

⅔ cup olive oil

⅓ cup red wine vinegar

THIS STRONG, SPICY HOMEMADE SLAW IS IDEAL ALONGSIDE TACOS, TORTAS AND SANDWICHES.

Combine all of the ingredients in a large bowl. Stir and toss well. Store in the refrigerator up to 2 days.

Aztecan Quinoa Salad

Serves 4 to 6

1½ cups quinoa

5 pickling cucumbers, peeled and cut into ¼-inch dice

1 small red onion, cut into ¼-inch dice

1 bunch Italian parsley, leaves only, chopped

2 bunches mint, leaves only, chopped

½ cup olive oil

¼ cup red wine vinegar

juice of 1 lemon

1½ teaspoons salt

¾ teaspoon freshly ground black pepper

6 romaine lettuce leaves

1 avocado, peeled, seeded and sliced, for garnish

Cracked Black Pepper Garnish, page 43 (optional)

Quinoa, a healthful high-protein grain, dates back to the Aztecs. The trick to eliminating its bitterness is to boil it in a generous quantity of water—and, whenever possible, buy organic. This refreshing salad, similar to tabbouleh, is best served the same day it is made. We are always partial to a large proportion of vegetable garnish to grain, as in this combination.

Bring 3 quarts of water to a boil in a large saucepan. Add the quinoa, stir once and return to a boil. Cook, uncovered, over moderate heat 10 minutes. Strain and rinse well with cold water. Shake the sieve well to remove all moisture.

When dry, transfer the quinoa to a large bowl. Add the remaining salad ingredients and toss well. Serve on lettuce-lined plates, topped with avocado slices and optional cracked pepper garnish.

CACTUS SALAD

Serves 4 to 6

1½ pounds fresh or prepared cactus paddles or nopales, needles removed

¾ cup olive oil

1½ teaspoons salt

4 Roma tomatoes, cored, seeded and cut into ¼-inch dice

½ small red onion, cut into ¼-inch dice

1 to 2 medium serrano chiles, stemmed, seeded and finely diced

2 bunches cilantro, leaves only, chopped

½ cup finely grated *Cotija* or *añejo* cheese

½ cup red wine vinegar

1 teaspoon freshly ground black pepper

4 to 6 red lettuce leaves

1 avocado, peeled, seeded and sliced, for garnish

¼ cup Cracked Black Pepper Garnish, page 43

GRILLING ENHANCES CACTUS'S STRONG VEGETABLE FLAVOR WITHOUT SOFTENING THE TEXTURE (WHICH HAPPENS TO BE MUCH MORE DELICIOUS FRESH THAN CANNED). THIS HEARTY SALAD MAKES A WONDERFUL STARTER OR ACCOMPANIMENT TO MOST LATIN MEALS, AS WELL AS A GREAT VEGETARIAN TACO WRAPPED IN A TORTILLA OR LETTUCE LEAF.

Preheat the grill or broiler.

Place the cactus paddles in a bowl and toss with ¼ cup of the olive oil and ½ teaspoon of the salt. Grill or broil the paddles until grill marks appear on each side, or they turn dark green with black patches, 3 to 5 minutes total. Set aside to cool to room temperature. Cover and chill 2 to 4 hours or overnight.

Cut the cactus into ½-inch pieces. In a large bowl, combine the cactus, tomatoes, onions, chiles, cilantro and cheese with the remaining ½ cup oil, the vinegar, the remaining 1 teaspoon salt and the pepper. Toss well. Serve on plates lined with lettuce leaves, and garnish with avocado slices sprinkled with cracked pepper garnish.

Seafood

In Mexico, where fresh fish and shellfish are abundant, they are often cooked quickly and simply. In keeping with that philosophy, here are some quick sautés for shrimp, squid and soft-shell crabs, along with an impressive, if a bit more complicated, oven-baked tortilla-wrapped fillet and a delicious sweet-and-sour octopus stew. We also have included several quick salsas for grilled fish that are a real boon to summer entertaining. They take no time to make and can be served either cold or at room temperature for maximum flexibility.

OCTOPUS VERACRUZANA

Serves 6 to 8

3½ cups fish stock or clam juice

½ cup golden raisins

¾ cup olive oil

1 medium white onion, thinly sliced

3 garlic cloves, chopped

3 Roma tomatoes, peeled, seeded and julienned

salt and freshly ground black pepper

2 medium red bell peppers, cored, seeded and julienned

2 medium yellow bell peppers, cored, seeded and julienned

2 medium poblano chiles, stemmed, seeded and julienned

2½ pounds baby or regular octopus, cleaned, blanched and cut into bite-sized pieces (see page 91)

1 bunch oregano, leaves only chopped

juice of 2 limes

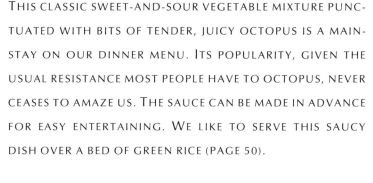

THIS CLASSIC SWEET-AND-SOUR VEGETABLE MIXTURE PUNCTUATED WITH BITS OF TENDER, JUICY OCTOPUS IS A MAINSTAY ON OUR DINNER MENU. ITS POPULARITY, GIVEN THE USUAL RESISTANCE MOST PEOPLE HAVE TO OCTOPUS, NEVER CEASES TO AMAZE US. THE SAUCE CAN BE MADE IN ADVANCE FOR EASY ENTERTAINING. WE LIKE TO SERVE THIS SAUCY DISH OVER A BED OF GREEN RICE (PAGE 50).

Combine the fish stock or clam juice and raisins in a small saucepan. Bring to a boil, reduce to a simmer and cook, uncovered, until the raisins are plump and light gold in color, 20 to 25 minutes. Transfer to a medium bowl and set aside.

In a large skillet heat 2 tablespoons of the olive oil over high heat. Sauté the onions 3 to 5 minutes until translucent and limp. Add the garlic and sauté about 30 seconds. Stir in the tomatoes with 1 teaspoon salt and ¾ teaspoon pepper and cook 2 to 3 minutes. Remove from the pan and set aside.

Sauté the peppers in the same skillet in 4 batches, adding 2 tablespoons of oil for each batch. The peppers should remain crisp and colorful, like a stir-fry. Transfer each finished batch to a platter to cool and then transfer to the bowl with raisins and stock. Add the tomato mixture. (The cooked vegetables can be refrigerated overnight if desired.)

In the same large skillet, heat the remaining 2 tablespoons oil over high heat until almost smoking. Sprinkle the cleaned octopus with salt and pepper. Sauté, stirring constantly, about 2 minutes.

Add the cooked vegetable mixture, oregano, lime juice and ¼ teaspoon each of salt and pepper. Stir and toss well to heat through and combine the flavors. Serve immediately over green rice.

SAUTÉED SHRIMP WITH ANCHO CHILES AND GARLIC

Serves 4

¾ cup olive oil

25 garlic cloves, peeled and thinly sliced

1¾ pounds rock or medium shrimp, peeled and deveined

1½ teaspoons salt

¾ teaspoon freshly ground black pepper

3 large ancho chiles, wiped clean, stemmed, seeded and finely julienned

1 cup fish stock or clam juice

juice of 3 large limes

1 bunch Italian parsley, leaves only, chopped

IN THIS TRADITIONAL ONE-SKILLET SUPPER, SLIVERED ANCHO CHILES AND GARLIC MAKE AN EASY YET DEEPLY FLAVORFUL SAUCE FOR QUICKLY COOKED SHRIMP. THOSE WHO PREFER THEIR MEXICAN FOOD ON THE LESS SPICY SIDE WILL ADORE THIS DISH.

Heat the olive oil in a large skillet over medium-low heat. Cook the garlic slices until tender but not brown. Transfer with a slotted spoon to paper towels and reserve.

Turn the heat under the pan up to high. Quickly toss the shrimp with the salt and pepper in a bowl. When the oil is nearly smoking, add the shrimp. Sauté, stirring and shaking the pan to prevent sticking, 3 to 4 minutes or just until the shrimp are still slightly undercooked. Remove from the heat. With a slotted spoon, transfer the shrimp to a platter, leaving as much liquid as possible in the pan.

Return the pan to the burner and reduce the heat to medium. Add the garlic slices and anchos and sauté, stirring frequently, until the oil begins to turn orange from the chiles. Stir in the fish stock or clam juice, along with the shrimp and any juice that has collected on the platter. Add the lime juice and parsley, bring to a boil and remove from the heat. Serve immediately over white rice.

SKEWERED MARINATED SALMON AND CUCUMBER

Serves 6

6 pickling cucumbers, ends trimmed and peeled

2 bunches cilantro, leaves only

3 ounces achiote paste (see page 6)

½ cup freshly squeezed orange juice

½ cup freshly squeezed lime juice

8 garlic cloves, roughly chopped

1½ tablespoons black peppercorns

2 pounds skinless salmon fillet

2 bunches red chard, stemmed and torn into large pieces

½ cup Lime Olive Oil Dressing, page 169

THESE PRETTY PINK AND WHITE SKEWERS ON THEIR BRIGHT BED OF BLANCHED CHARD ARE A NICE, EASY CHOICE FOR SUMMER PARTIES. THESE CAN BE MADE SMALLER AND SERVED AS A GREAT COCKTAIL PARTY HORS D'OEUVRE.

Cut the cucumbers in half lengthwise and then slice across the width into ½-inch half-moons. Sprinkle with salt and let sit in a colander for 20 to 30 minutes.

Combine the cilantro, achiote, orange juice, lime juice, garlic and peppercorns in a blender. Puree until smooth.

Cut the salmon into 1½-inch chunks and place in a nonreactive bowl. Pour over the cilantro marinade and let sit 20 to 30 minutes.

Preheat the grill or broiler.

Bring a large pot of salted water to a boil and blanch the chard just until wilted. Drain, transfer to a bowl of iced water and then drain again. Squeeze out any excess water. Transfer to a large bowl and toss with the lime dressing.

Thread alternating salmon and cucumber chunks on skewers. Grill or broil about 1½ minutes per side. Line a serving platter or plates with the chard. Top with the skewers and serve.

PANFRIED SPICED SHRIMP

Serves 2

¹/₂ teaspoon salt

¹/₂ teaspoon freshly ground black pepper

1 teaspoon ground cumin

1 teaspoon paprika

8 ounces medium shrimp or prawns in the shell, washed

2 tablespoons olive oil

1 red jalapeño chile or small red bell pepper, stemmed, seeded and julienned

1 large scallion, trimmed and thinly sliced on the diagonal

1 garlic clove, thinly sliced

juice of 1 lime

TO GET THE MOST FROM THIS GREAT SPICY SHRIMP DISH, ALL YOU NEED IS PERFECTLY FRESH MEDIUM-SIZED SHRIMPS OR PRAWNS (PREFERABLY WITH THEIR HEADS ON), A NONSTICK SKILLET, ABOUT FIVE MINUTES AT THE STOVE—AND THE KIND OF COMPANION YOU CAN FREELY SUCK ON SHRIMP SHELLS WITH.

Combine the salt, pepper, cumin and paprika in a bowl. Add the shrimp and toss to coat evenly.

Heat the oil in a large skillet over high heat. Sauté the shrimp 1 to 2 minutes. Toss in the jalapeño or bell pepper, scallion and garlic and cook 1 minute longer. Remove from the heat, stir in the lime juice and serve.

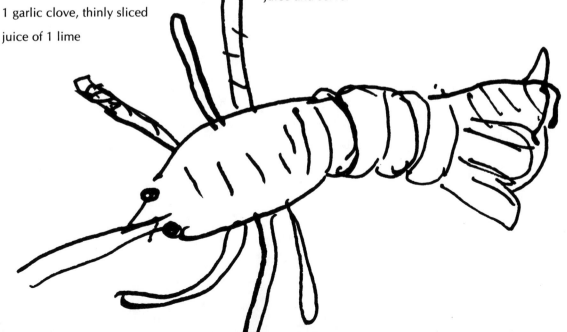

SOFT-SHELL CRABS WITH TOMATILLOS AND BROWN BUTTER

Serves 2

2 large live soft-shell crabs

1 1/2 teaspoons salt

1 teaspoon freshly ground black pepper

flour for dredging

4 tablespoons unsalted butter

2 tomatillos, husked, washed and diced

1/2 jalapeño chile, stemmed, seeded and minced

1/2 bunch cilantro, leaves only, chopped

juice of 1 lime

IN THIS LATIN VARIATION ON THE CLASSIC BROWN BUTTER AND CAPERS THEME, TOMATILLOS, JALAPEÑOS AND LIME JUICE BEAUTIFULLY CUT THE RICHNESS OF SOFT-SHELL CRABS. WE LIKE TO COOK THE LIVE CRABS UNCLEANED— WITH ALL THEIR LITTLE PARTS INTACT—READY TO SPEW FORTH JUICES AS SOON AS THEY HIT THE PAN.

Wipe the crabs clean with a dry towel and remove any packing straw. Season the crabs evenly on both sides with 1 teaspoon of the salt and 1/2 teaspoon pepper. Dip the crabs in the flour to coat and then pat off excess.

Melt the butter in a nonstick pan over medium-high heat. Cook the crabs, with their backs down first, 1 1/2 minutes per side, being cautious of splattering butter. Transfer the crabs to a platter.

Add the tomatillos and jalapeño to the pan and cook over high heat until well browned, about 1 minute. Remove from the heat and stir in the cilantro, lime juice, and remaining 1/2 teaspoon each salt and pepper. Place the crabs on serving plates, spoon on the sauce and serve immediately.

SQUID SAUTÉ WITH TOMATOES AND GARLIC

**Serves 4 as an entrée,
6 as an appetizer**

1½ pounds squid, cleaned

15 garlic cloves, peeled

½ cup olive oil

1 teaspoon salt

1 teaspoon freshly ground black pepper

2 large tomatoes, peeled, seeded and diced

1 large bunch oregano, leaves only, chopped

THIS DISH WORKS BEST WHEN THE SQUID IS SAUTÉED IN BATCHES. IF THE PAN GETS TOO CROWDED, IT STEAMS RATHER THAN SAUTÉS, WHICH TOUGHENS THE MEAT.

Cut the squid into ¼-inch rings. Wash, dry and place in a mixing bowl.

Puree the garlic with ¼ cup of the olive oil in a blender until smooth. Pour over the squid. Add the salt and pepper, tossing well to combine.

Heat a dry medium skillet over high heat. Then add a generous tablespoon of the remaining olive oil and heat until almost smoking. Pour in one-third of the marinated squid and sauté about 30 seconds. Stir in one-third each of the tomatoes and oregano and cook about 2 minutes longer, just until the tomatoes dissolve and the garlic colors slightly. Transfer to a platter, wipe out the skillet and repeat two times. Serve hot over rice and beans as an entrée, or with flour tortillas as an appetizer.

BAby Squid

TORTILLA-WRAPPED FISH

Serves 6

6 tablespoons olive oil

2 cups diced, peeled Yukon Gold potatoes

2 medium yellow onions, diced

4 garlic cloves, minced

2 ripe tomatoes, cored, seeded and diced

1 bunch oregano, leaves only, chopped

1 cup chopped pitted green olives

½ teaspoon freshly ground black pepper, plus more to taste

juice of 2 limes

½ cup vegetable oil

18 small Corn Tortillas, page 132

6 (6-ounce) red snapper or sea bass fillets, about 1 inch thick, washed and dried

salt to taste

2 limes, cut into thick wedges, for garnish

IN THIS RUSTIC DISH, THE TORTILLAS BOTH ADD FLAVOR AND SEAL IN MOISTURE, FORCING ALL THE ELEMENTS TO MARRY AND GROW MORE INTENSE. GRILLING IS PREFERABLE, IF YOU HAVE THE TIME, SINCE IT ADDS YET ANOTHER LAYER OF FLAVOR.

Heat the olive oil in a large skillet over high heat. Sauté the potatoes, shaking the pan frequently, until golden brown, 5 to 7 minutes. Transfer with a slotted spoon to a mixing bowl. Then sauté the onions in the oil about 5 minutes. Add the garlic and sauté 1 minute more. Add the tomatoes and oregano and cook an additional minute. Remove from the heat and stir in the olives. Add to the potatoes in the bowl. Add the pepper, stir well to combine and set aside.

Heat the grill or preheat the oven to 450°F.

In another medium skillet, heat the vegetable oil until hot but not smoking. Using tongs, dip each tortilla in the oil, and cook 30 seconds per side. Drain on paper towels.

Liberally season the fish fillets all over with salt and pepper.

Place a 14-inch length of aluminum foil on the counter. Arrange 3 tortillas on the foil so they overlap in the center to form a triangle. Place a fish fillet in the center. Divide the potato mixture into 6 parts and mound 1 portion evenly over the fillet. Fold over the tortillas to enclose the stuffing and form a triangle and then wrap with the foil to seal the packet. Repeat with the remaining fillets.

To grill, cook 9 minutes per side on a moderately hot spot on the grill. To bake, place the packets directly on an oven rack and cook 20 to 25 minutes. (Unwrap a packet to check for doneness by flaking the fish.)

To serve, unwrap and discard the foil and, with a spatula, transfer the tortilla-wrapped fish to dinner plates. Open out the tortillas to resemble the petals of a flower. Though they may be eaten, the real purpose of the tortillas is to add moisture and flavor. Serve with plenty of thick lime wedges as garnish.

SCALLOPS POACHED IN ACHIOTE SAUCE

Serves 4 to 6

4 tablespoons unsalted butter

1 onion, sliced

1 teaspoon salt

4 garlic cloves, roughly chopped

3 ounces achiote paste (see page 6)

½ cup white vinegar

2 tablespoons tomato paste

2 cups fish stock or clam juice

1½ teaspoons black peppercorns, crushed

2 pounds sea scallops, muscle removed, or rock shrimp

½ cup capers or Pickled Red Onions, page 46, for garnish

FOR AN EVEN SILKIER SAUCE, YOU CAN STIR IN TWO OR THREE TABLESPOONS OF BUTTER AT THE LAST MINUTE.

Melt the butter in a medium saucepan over moderate heat. Sauté the onions with the salt until caramelized, about 10 minutes. Add the garlic and achiote paste and cook 5 minutes, stirring frequently with a wooden spoon to avoid scorching. Add the tomato paste and pour in the fish stock or clam juice and boil 5 minutes longer. Stir in the pepper and vinegar and remove from the heat.

Transfer the sauce to a blender and puree. Pass through a strainer. (The sauce keeps up to 4 days.)

To finish, pour the sauce into a large skillet. Bring to a boil over high heat. Stir in the scallops or shrimp, reduce the heat to medium and cook 3 to 5 minutes. Serve over a bed of white rice and garnish with the capers or pickled onions.

pepper

ROASTED PEPPER COMPOTE FOR FISH

**Makes 1 1/2 cups,
enough for 4 servings**

2 red bell peppers, roasted, peeled,
seeded (see page 11) and julienned

2 yellow bell peppers, roasted, peeled,
seeded (see page 11) and julienned

2 poblano chiles or green bell peppers,
roasted, peeled, seeded (see page 11) and
julienned

1 large bunch oregano, leaves only,
chopped

1 small red onion, thinly sliced

1/2 cup olive oil

juice of 2 limes or 1/4 cup red wine
vinegar

1 teaspoon salt

1/2 teaspoon freshly ground black pepper

OUR EASY MIXTURE OF ROASTED PEPPER STRIPS IS ALSO
GOOD AS A SIDE DISH OR SERVED OVER SALAD GREENS OR A
WARM HUNK OF FETA CHEESE. IT IS SUSAN'S FAVORITE QUICK
SAUCE.

Mix all of the ingredients in a large bowl. Let sit 4 to 5 hours to
develop the flavors, or serve at once.

To serve, spread on a platter or serving plates and top with grilled,
broiled or sautéed fish fillets.

Olive and Oregano Compote for Fish

Makes about 2¹/₂ cups, enough for 4 servings

¹/₂ cup plus ¹/₃ cup olive oil

1 onion, thinly sliced

20 garlic cloves, sliced paper-thin

1 teaspoon salt

1 jalapeño chile, stemmed, seeded if desired and minced

¹/₂ cup chopped capers

¹/₂ cup chopped pitted green olives

2 Roma tomatoes, cored, seeded and chopped

1 bunch oregano, leaves only, chopped

¹/₃ cup red wine vinegar

2 teaspoons honey

STRONGLY FLAVORED FRESH COMPOTES LIKE THIS ONE ARE SUCH A NATURAL COMPLEMENT FOR GRILLED FISH IT IS DIFFICULT TO IMAGINE WANTING TO COOK ANYTHING MORE COMPLEX—ESPECIALLY IN THE SUMMERTIME.

Heat ¹/₂ cup of the oil in a skillet over medium-low heat. Sauté the onions and garlic with the salt until soft but not brown, 5 to 7 minutes. Set aside to cool 10 minutes.

Transfer the onion mixture to a bowl. Add the remaining ingredients and mix well. The compote can be refrigerated overnight. Serve with roasted or grilled fish.

RED, WHITE AND BLACK BEAN SALSA FOR FISH

Makes about 3 cups, enough for 4 servings

½ cup dried black beans

½ cup dried red kidney or pinto beans

½ cup dried white beans (Great Northern or cannellini)

1 small red onion, finely diced

1 bunch cilantro, leaves only, roughly chopped

½ cup olive oil

¾ teaspoon salt

½ teaspoon freshly ground black pepper

3 tablespoons juice from Pickled Chipotles (or moritas), page 46, or red wine vinegar

1 Pickled Chipotle (or morita) Chile, page 46, seeded if desired and minced

IN OUR QUEST FOR UNFUSSY SAUCES, WE CAME UP WITH THIS KNOCKOUT SPICY BEAN SALSA. FOR THE BEST RESULTS, START WITH ORGANIC BEANS AND TOSS WITH THE DRESSING WHILE THE BEANS ARE STILL HOT SO THEY ABSORB MAXIMUM FLAVOR. SMOKING THE BEANS, THOUGH NOT ESSENTIAL, ADDS ANOTHER DELIGHTFUL LAYER OF FLAVOR.

Keeping them separate, wash and pick over all the beans. Place each kind in a separate pot, cover generously with water and bring to a boil. Reduce the heat to medium-low and cook, covered, until the beans are done in the center but not too soft, 1 to 1½ hours. Drain and rinse in a colander.

For added flavor, you can smoke the beans on a grill. Start a small fire off to one side and throw soaked wood chips on the coals when the fire is moderately hot. Lay out the beans on a baking pan, pour in water to a depth of ⅛ inch and cover with a wet towel. Place on the grate, cover and smoke 2 hours, adding more wood chips every 20 minutes or so. Set aside to cool and then drain.

Transfer the beans to a large mixing bowl. Add the remaining ingredients and mix well. Bean salsa can be refrigerated up to 2 days. Bring back to room temperature before serving.

To serve, line a platter or serving plates with salsa and top with grilled, broiled or sautéed fish fillets.

TOMATILLO RELISH FOR GRILLED FISH

**Makes 4³/₄ cups,
enough for 8 servings**

1 pound tomatillos, husked, washed and chopped

1 pound Roma tomatoes, cored and chopped

1 large onion, chopped

½ cup olive oil

⅓ cup white vinegar

1 bunch cilantro, leaves only, chopped

¼ cup sugar

6 garlic cloves, minced

1 jalapeño chile, stemmed, seeded and diced

1 red bell pepper, cored, seeded and chopped

2 teaspoons salt

1 teaspoon freshly ground black pepper

TOMATILLO RELISH, A CINCH TO MAKE ONCE THE VEGETA-
BLES ARE CHOPPED, RESEMBLES A SWEET-AND-SOUR MEXI-
CAN RATATOUILLE. WITH ITS ASSERTIVE CHARACTER, IT
PROVIDES A REFRESHING CONTRAST TO MILD-TASTING FISH.
IT ALSO GOES WELL WITH COLD MEATS.

Combine all the ingredients in a pot, cover and simmer about 1 hour. Set aside to cool to room temperature. Tomatillo relish can be stored in the refrigerator up to a week.

To serve, line a large platter or serving plates with relish and top with grilled fish fillets. Or serve as a condiment with cold meats. Garnish with grilled scallions.

Poultry

Since chicken is such a popular item at the restaurant, we are always on the lookout for new and enticing preparations. Some of our current favorites, besides the juiciest roasted and grilled chicken recipes known to mankind, are an easy green mole based on roasted pumpkin seeds, fragrant banana leaf–wrapped chicken pibil from the Yucatán and simple, delicious marinated Cornish game hens.

Roast Achiote Citrus Chicken

Serves 4

Achiote Citrus Marinade, recipe follows

1 (3-pound) roasting chicken, rinsed and patted dry

1 onion, peeled

1 head garlic

1 orange

Our citrus-garlic-spice marinade produces a moist, flavorful bird with a beautiful brown skin. This is the chicken we use for tacos and panuchos.

Rub the marinade all over the chicken, inside and out. Place in a bowl, cover and refrigerate at least 1 hour or as long as overnight.

Preheat the oven to 400°F.

Lift the chicken from the marinade and place on a work surface. Cut the onion, head of garlic and orange in half and stuff inside the chicken's cavity. Tie the legs together and place on a rack in a roasting pan, breast side down.

Roast 20 minutes, then reduce the heat to 350°F and roast 20 minutes longer. Turn the chicken, breast side up, and bake 40 to 50 minutes longer, basting occasionally with the pan juices, until a drumstick feels loose when jiggled and the skin is golden brown. Remove from the oven and let sit 10 minutes before serving. Serve warm with rice and beans.

ACHIOTE CITRUS MARINADE

**Makes 1¹/₂ cups, enough for
1 roasting chicken or 1¹/₂
pounds chicken legs and thighs**

²/₃ cup freshly squeezed orange juice

¹/₄ cup achiote paste (see page 6)

2 to 3 jalapeño chiles, stemmed and
seeded if desired

7 garlic cloves, peeled

1 tablespoon black peppercorns

1 tablespoon salt

1 bunch cilantro, stems and leaves

Combine ¹/₃ cup of the orange juice, the achiote paste, jalapeños, garlic, peppercorns and salt in a blender or food processor. Puree until the peppercorns are completely crushed. Add the cilantro and the remaining ¹/₃ cup orange juice and puree until smooth.

VARIATION

FOR CHICKEN CHUNKS OR SHREDS FOR TACOS AND PANUCHOS, MARINATE 1¹/₂ POUNDS CHICKEN LEGS AND THIGHS IN THE SAME MANNER. BAKE IN A ROASTING PAN OR A BAKING SHEET IN A 350°F OVEN FOR 40 MINUTES, OR UNTIL THE MEAT EASILY PULLS AWAY FROM THE BONE. SET THE CHICKEN ASIDE TO COOL AND POUR THE COOKING JUICES FROM THE PAN INTO A BOWL OR CUP. REFRIGERATE THE JUICES SO THE FAT RISES TO THE TOP.

WHEN THE CHICKEN IS COOL, REMOVE AND DISCARD THE SKIN AND BONES AND CUT OR SHRED THE MEAT INTO BITE-SIZED PIECES. (SUSAN, A FEARLESS SKIN EATER, RECOMMENDS CHOPPING IT UP AND ADDING IT TO THE SHRED-DED CHICKEN FOR AN EXTRA DOLLOP OF FLAVOR.) SKIM OFF AND DISCARD THE FAT THAT HAS RISEN FROM THE COOKING JUICES, AND USE THE REMAIN-ING BROWN COOKING LIQUID TO REHEAT THE CHICKEN IN A SLOW OVEN.

CHICKEN AL CARBÓN WITH ORANGE CILANTRO SALSA

Serves 6

6 whole chicken breasts, boneless but with skin on

Spicy Citrus Marinade, recipe follows

Orange Cilantro Salsa, recipe follows

THE TRICK TO GRILLING ANY CITRUS-MARINATED CHICKEN IS TO MOVE IT AWAY FROM DIRECT HEAT AFTER IT IS SEARED TO PREVENT THE SUGARS FROM BLACKENING WHILE THE INTERIOR COOKS THROUGH. (ON THE OTHER HAND, BURNT SPOTS CAN EASILY BE CAMOUFLAGED WITH A DOLLOP OF THE ORANGE SALSA.) THIS MARINADE PRODUCES AN EXCEPTIONALLY JUICY AND FLAVORFUL GRILLED CHICKEN. WE LIKE TO SERVE IT OVER A BED OF RED RICE (PAGE 51) WITH A SIDE OF REFRIED BLACK BEANS (PAGE 53).

Wash the chicken breasts and place in a large stainless steel or plastic container. Pour on the marinade, cover and refrigerate at least 6 hours, or overnight.

Preheat the grill or broiler until very hot.

Grill the chicken breasts, skin side down on the grill, or skin side up in the broiler, 2 to 3 minutes. Then turn and cook the other side. Keep turning the chicken every minute or 2 to avoid blackening or sticking; total cooking time is 10 to 12 minutes for small breasts and 18 to 20 for larger breasts. (We always cook chicken breasts with the skin on for flavor. For skinless chicken, we just remove it before serving.)

Serve hot on top of red rice and black beans. Top with the orange cilantro salsa.

SPICY CITRUS MARINADE

Makes 2 cups

1 cup freshly squeezed orange juice

2 tablespoons freshly squeezed lime juice

1 morita chile or 3 árbol chiles

1 cup Red Tomato Salsa, page 36

1/4 cup vegetable oil

1/2 teaspoon salt

Combine the orange juice, lime juice and chile(s) in a small saucepan and bring to a boil. Reduce to a simmer and cook, uncovered, until the chile is plump, about 5 minutes. Set aside to cool.

Transfer the citrus mixture to a blender. Add the remaining ingredients and puree until smooth.

ORANGE CILANTRO SALSA

Makes about 1 1/2 to 2 cups

4 oranges, peeled and sectioned

1 bunch cilantro, leaves and stems, roughly chopped

1 small jalapeño chile, stemmed, seeded and finely diced

1 small red onion, julienned

1/4 cup olive oil

1/4 cup red wine vinegar

1 teaspoon salt

1/2 teaspoon cracked black pepper

Combine the oranges, cilantro, jalapeño, onion, olive oil, red wine vinegar, salt and pepper. Mix well and set aside.

PUMPKIN SEED CHICKEN MOLE

Serves 4 to 6

½ cup raw pumpkin seeds or pepitas

1 teaspoon cumin seeds

½ teaspoon cracked black pepper

½ teaspoon dried Mexican oregano

10 tomatillos, husked, washed and quartered

1 serrano chile

2 garlic cloves, peeled

2 romaine lettuce leaves

⅛ teaspoon ground cinnamon

1 bunch cilantro, stems and leaves

2 radish tops

1 small onion, quartered

1½ teaspoons salt

2 tablespoons olive oil

2 cups chicken stock

3 large skinless, boneless chicken breasts, split

1 bunch radishes, thinly sliced, for garnish

MOLES ARE ONE OF THE GREAT MISUNDERSTOOD DISHES OF THE MEXICAN KITCHEN. THERE ARE HUNDREDS OF VARIATIONS ON THE THEME OF GROUND SEEDS, NUTS, HERBS, SPICES AND VEGETABLES STEWED TOGETHER IN A RICH SAUCE WITH PIECES OF CHICKEN OR MEATS, BUT FOR SOME REASON THE ONE THAT HAS TRAVELED BEST IS THE BROWN ONE, THE ONE SEASONED WITH CHOCOLATE. OUR REFRESHING GREEN MOLE BEARS LITTLE RESEMBLANCE TO THAT CHOCOLATE-COVERED CHICKEN. IT IS LIGHT AND AROMATIC AND CAN BE PUT TOGETHER IN RECORD TIME FOR A MOLE.

Place a dry cast-iron skillet over low heat. Toast the pumpkin seeds, cumin seeds, pepper and oregano, shaking the pan occasionally, until their aromas are released, about 5 minutes. Do not brown. Set aside to cool and then grind in a blender or food processor to a powder. Reserve.

Combine the tomatillos, serrano chile, garlic, lettuce, cinnamon, cilantro, radish tops, onion and salt in a food processor. Puree until smooth.

Preheat the oven to 350°F.

Heat the olive oil in a large saucepan over high heat. Standing back to avoid splatters, pour in the pureed tomatillo mixture, and sizzle for 30 seconds. Stir in the stock, reduce the heat and simmer 10 minutes. Turn the heat up to high and bring to a boil. Stir in the ground nut mixture and remove from the heat. Puree in a food processor or blender, in batches if necessary. Pass through a fine strainer, pressing with the back of a ladle to extract all the juices, into a 13 × 10-inch flameproof baking dish.

Place the chicken breasts in the sauce and bring to a boil over moderate heat. Cover with foil, transfer to the oven and bake 20 minutes. Serve the chicken and sauce over a bed of white rice. Sprinkle the radish slices over the top.

PANFRIED CHICKEN WITH ANCHO CHILES AND MUSHROOMS

Serves 6

8 tablespoons (1 stick) unsalted butter

1 medium onion, sliced

salt and freshly ground black pepper

2 to 4 garlic cloves, sliced

½ pound oyster mushrooms, cleaned and sliced

½ pound white mushrooms, cleaned and sliced

1 cup dry white wine

3 to 4 dried ancho chiles, wiped clean, stemmed and seeded

2½ cups chicken stock

juice of 1 lime

¼ cup olive oil

3 large whole boneless chicken breasts with skin, split

AFTER WORKING MOSTLY WITH FRESH GREEN CHILES, WE WERE IMPRESSED BY THE PURE CHILE FLAVOR OF DRIED CHILES LIKE ANCHOS. WE CHOSE THEM FOR THIS ELEGANT EUROPEAN-STYLE ENTRÉE BECAUSE, ALONG WITH THE MUSHROOMS, THEY CREATE A SAUCE OF MANY TEXTURES AND TASTES. ALL SUCH A FULL-BODIED DISH NEEDS IS WHITE RICE AND A SIMPLE GREEN VEGETABLE FOR ACCOMPANIMENTS.

Melt 4 tablespoons of the butter in a medium saucepan over moderate heat. Sauté the onions with ½ teaspoon each of salt and pepper until golden brown, 8 to 10 minutes. Add the garlic and half of each of the mushrooms. Turn up the heat and cook the mushrooms, stirring frequently, until golden. Pour in the wine and cook until most of the liquid has evaporated.

Meanwhile, place the ancho chiles over a burner and toast all over just until soft and the skin is slightly bubbly. Roughly chop half the chiles and add to the pot, reserving the rest.

Add the chicken stock to the pot and boil about 12 minutes. Transfer to a blender or food processor and puree until smooth. (For a smoother sauce, pass through a sieve.) Return the sauce to the stove and bring to a boil. Stir in the remaining butter, 1 tablespoon at a time, and remove from heat. (For a thinner, more rustic sauce you can eliminate this butter.) Stir in the lime juice, season with salt and pepper and reserve.

Preheat the oven to 350°F.

Season the chicken breasts well with salt and pepper. Heat a large dry skillet over moderate heat for 5 minutes. Pour in the olive

oil and place the chicken in the pan, skin side down. Fry until the skin starts to brown and crisp, 5 to 10 minutes, and then turn and briefly sear the other side. Transfer to a baking dish (set the pan aside) and bake until cooked through, about 10 minutes.

Meanwhile, finish the sauce by thinly slicing the remaining toasted ancho peppers. Reheat the pan used to brown the chicken and sauté the remaining mushrooms over medium-high heat until the edges are brown. Then add the sliced anchos and stir and toss 1 to 2 minutes longer. Stir into the reserved sauce.

Coat the serving plates with the sauce. Top each with a browned chicken breast and serve.

CHICKEN PIBIL

Serves 6

¼ cup achiote paste (see page 6)

10 garlic cloves, peeled

2 teaspoons cumin seeds

¼ teaspoon ground cinnamon

½ cup freshly squeezed orange juice

¼ cup freshly squeezed lime juice

¼ cup red wine vinegar

1½ teaspoons salt

2 teaspoons cracked black pepper

6 chicken legs with thighs, ankle joint removed and scored to the bone and skin removed

2 medium onions, cut into 3 slices each, plus 2 medium onions, diced

3 Roma tomatoes, cut into 4 slices each

6 banana leaves (optional), cut into 10-inch squares and toasted over a burner about 2 seconds per side to soften

3 tablespoons unsalted butter

2 cups chicken stock

IN THE TRADITIONAL YUCATECAN VERSION OF THIS DISH, CHICKEN OR PORK IS MARINATED IN A RICH ACHIOTE-TINGED SAUCE, WRAPPED IN BANANA LEAVES AND THEN SLOW-COOKED IN AN EARTHEN PIT. WE'VE MODERNIZED THINGS A BIT BY USING THE OVEN AND MAKING A SEPARATE SAUCE, BUT THE RESULTS ARE STILL TENDER AND DEEPLY SATISFYING. THE BANANA LEAVES SEAL IN MOISTURE AND ADD A SUBTLE GRASSY NOTE, BUT IF THEY ARE UNAVAILABLE, BLANCHED COLLARD GREENS ARE A GOOD SUBSTITUTE.

Combine the achiote paste, garlic, cumin, cinnamon, orange and lime juices, vinegar, salt and pepper in a blender. Puree until smooth. Pour into a nonreactive baking pan, add the chicken and turn to coat. Cover and marinate in the refrigerator at least 2 or up to 24 hours.

Preheat the oven to 375°F.

Heat a dry cast-iron skillet over high heat. Char the onion slices until blackened on both sides. Then char the tomato slices on both sides. Reserve.

Cut six 16 × 14-inch sheets of heavy-duty aluminum foil. If using banana leaves, place 1 on top of each piece of foil. Center a piece of chicken on each, reserving the marinade. Top each with 2 tomato slices and 1 slice of onion. Wrap and seal the banana leaf and the foil to enclose. Place on a baking sheet. Transfer to the oven and bake 45 minutes.

Meanwhile, melt the butter in a medium saucepan over medium-high heat. Sauté the diced onions until golden brown. Stir in the reserved marinade, bring to a boil and cook, stirring frequently, 5 minutes. Add the chicken stock and cook 10 minutes longer. Reserve.

When the chicken is ready, remove from the oven and open the packets. Transfer the chicken, with the banana leaves if using, to serving plates. Pour any excess juice from the pan into the sauce. Pour the hot sauce over the chicken and serve with rice, beans and Pickled Red Onions (page 46).

Drunken Chicken

Serves 6

3 pasilla chiles, wiped clean, stemmed and seeded

1 cup freshly squeezed orange juice

2 cups chicken stock

3 tablespoons vegetable oil

1 large onion, diced

salt and freshly ground black pepper

1 pound bulk chorizo sausage

½ cup gold tequila

6 boneless chicken breast halves, with skin

1 bunch cilantro, leaves only, for garnish

½ cup chopped red onion, for garnish

This voluptuous marriage of chicken, sausage and tequila was created for a special Valentine's Day menu. It would be lovely with white rice and fried plantains and nothing more than a simple passion fruit sorbet for dessert.

Lightly toast the chiles over an open flame. Place in a blender with the orange juice and chicken stock. Puree until smooth and reserve.

Heat 1 tablespoon of the oil in a medium skillet over medium-low heat. Cook the onions with 1 teaspoon salt and ½ teaspoon pepper until golden, 8 to 10 minutes. Add the chorizo, stirring often to break up the sausage, and cook about 10 minutes, or until the onions are golden brown and the meat is cooked through. Strain, discarding the fat, and return to the pan. Pour in the tequila, turn up the heat and cook until reduced by half. (Be careful, as the tequila may flame.) Pour in the pureed chile mixture. Bring to a boil, reduce to a simmer and cook 10 minutes. Remove from the heat and reserve.

Preheat the oven to 350°F.

Heat the remaining 2 tablespoons vegetable oil in an ovenproof skillet over medium-high heat. Season the chicken breasts all over with salt and pepper. Sauté, skin side down, about 4 minutes, shaking the pan frequently to prevent sticking. Then turn and sauté the other side 4 minutes. Pour on the reserved chorizo sauce, transfer to the oven and bake 12 minutes. Serve hot over rice. Garnish generously with the cilantro leaves and chopped onion.

GAME HENS WITH LIME, GARLIC AND OREGANO

Serves 2 to 4

4 limes, 3 juiced and 1 halved

8 garlic cloves, minced

1 tablespoon dried Mexican oregano, crushed

2 tablespoons olive oil

2 Rock Cornish hens, washed and patted dry

1 bunch oregano

1 onion, peeled and cut into chunks

salt and freshly ground black pepper

HERBS

THIS IS THE KIND OF SIMPLE FOOD WE LIKE TO COOK AND EAT AT HOME. MARY SUE, WHO IS PARTIAL TO SMALL BIRDS FOR THEIR MEATIER FLAVOR, ALSO LIKES TO ROAST THEM ON THE GRILL BY PLACING THEM IN A PAN AWAY FROM THE DIRECT HEAT, COVERING THE GRILL AND COOKING, ROTATING THE PAN EVERY SO OFTEN, FOR ABOUT AN HOUR.

In a small bowl, mix the juice of the 3 limes, garlic, dried oregano and olive oil. Rub all over the hens and set in the refrigerator 1 to 2 hours.

Preheat the oven to 375°F.

Remove the hens from the refrigerator. Stuff the cavity of each with half of the fresh oregano, a lime half and half of the onion chunks. Tie the legs together with string and sprinkle all over with salt and pepper. Place on a rack in a roasting pan and roast, breast side up, 20 minutes. Turn breast side down and roast another 20 minutes. Then turn over again and roast 20 minutes longer (1 hour total). Serve hot.

GRILLED TURKEY BREAST WITH VINEGAR AND CRACKED PEPPER

Serves 6

2¼ pounds raw turkey breast, cut into thin scallops

salt and freshly ground black pepper

olive oil for brushing

7½ tablespoons unsalted butter, cold

2 medium red onions, diced

1 cup white vinegar

2 cups turkey or chicken stock or canned broth

1 tablespoon cracked black pepper

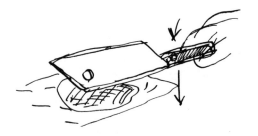

FRESHLY CRACKED RATHER THAN PRECRACKED PEPPER-CORNS MAKE A HUGE DIFFERENCE IN THIS DISH SINCE THE PEPPER IS MORE A FEATURED INGREDIENT THAN A MERE SEASONING. A GREAT FAST ENTRÉE FOR ENTERTAINING, THIS WOULD MAKE A TERRIFIC NONTRADITIONAL TURKEY DINNER WITH SEARED GREENS (PAGE 56) AND BAKED YAMS WITH LIME AND HONEY (PAGE 58).

Cover the turkey slices with plastic wrap and pound to flatten. Sprinkle all over with salt and pepper, brush lightly with olive oil and reserve.

Preheat the grill or broiler.

Melt 3 tablespoons of the butter in a medium skillet over low heat. Cook the onions with 1½ teaspoons salt, stirring and shaking the pan frequently, until the onions are golden, about 15 minutes. Pour in the vinegar, turn the heat up to high and reduce by half. Then pour in the turkey or chicken stock and reduce again by half.

Thinly slice the remaining cold butter. Reduce the heat to low and whisk the butter into the sauce a little at a time. Remove from the heat. Stir in the cracked pepper.

Grill or broil the turkey slices less than a minute per side. Serve over a bed of seared greens, if desired, with the sauce over all.

ROAST DUCK
WITH CHIPOTLE GLAZE

Serves 2 for dinner, 4 for lunch

2 cups freshly squeezed orange juice

½ cup honey

1 cup chipotle pickling juice (see page 46) or red wine vinegar

salt and freshly ground black pepper

1 (5-pound) duck, halved and backbone removed

SIMPLY ROASTED DUCK IS A WONDERFUL DISH WHEN YOU DON'T FEEL LIKE FUSSING WITH A SAUCE BUT STILL WANT SOMETHING SPECIAL. THE FRUITY CHIPOTLE GLAZE PRODUCES A GREAT BROWN, CRUSTY SKIN.

To make the glaze, combine the orange juice, honey, chipotle pickling juice or red wine vinegar, 1½ teaspoons salt and ½ teaspoon pepper in a small saucepan. Bring to a boil and cook until reduced by one fourth, about 5 to 6 minutes. Set aside to cool.

Preheat the oven to 425°F.

Season the duck all over with salt and pepper. Place skin side up on a rack in a roasting pan. Roast 30 minutes, then reduce the heat to 375°F and roast 45 minutes longer.

Remove from the oven and generously brush with the glaze. Return to the oven and continue roasting 30 minutes longer, generously brushing with the remaining glaze every 10 minutes. Cut each piece in half and serve hot with any remaining glaze for dipping.

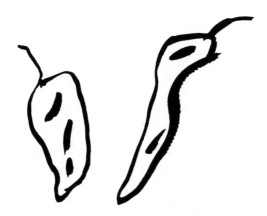

BRAISED DUCK WITH
SPICED LENTILS AND LIME ONIONS

Serves 4

1 (5-pound) duck

2 teaspoons salt

1½ teaspoons freshly ground black pepper

2 garlic cloves, crushed

2 cinnamon sticks, halved

4 cups chicken or duck fat or lard

⅓ cup olive oil

2 onions, thinly sliced

½ cup freshly squeezed lime juice

1 recipe Spiced Pineapple Lentils, page 65, warmed

THE TRADITIONAL FRENCH CONFIT METHOD IS OUR FAVORITE WAY TO COOK DUCK BECAUSE THE MEAT STAYS SO MOIST AND FLAVORFUL. DON'T LET THE QUANTITY OF FAT SCARE YOU—VERY LITTLE REMAINS ON THE MEAT ONCE THE DUCK IS COOKED. ALL OF THE COMPONENTS OF THIS DISH, INCLUDING THE PUNGENT LIME ONIONS, CAN BE MADE IN ADVANCE.

Cut the duck in quarters and remove the drumstick tips. Season with 1 teaspoon each of the salt and pepper, rub all over with the garlic and place a piece of cinnamon stick on each quarter. Let sit at room temperature 45 minutes.

Preheat the oven to 350°F.

Transfer the duck to an ovenproof frying pan along with the chicken or other fat. Bring to a boil over medium-high heat, cover with foil and transfer to the oven. Bake 1 hour and 15 minutes. Set aside to cool.

When cool enough to handle, lift the duck from the fat and remove and discard the skin. Cover with a wet towel until serving time. To reserve, store the duck in the cooking fat and refrigerate up to a week.

To reheat the duck, remove from the fat if necessary, and place on a rack in a tightly covered pan. Warm in a 325°F oven for about 15 minutes.

Meanwhile, to make the lime onions, heat the olive oil in a medium skillet over high heat. Sauté the onions, stirring frequently, until just wilted (but not browned). Toss with the lime juice and the remaining 1 teaspoon salt and ½ teaspoon pepper. Keep warm. The onions can be made a day in advance and refrigerated. Reheat before serving.

To serve, spread a bed of lentils on each serving plate. Top with a piece of duck and smother with the warm onions. Serve immediately.

Meats

IF YOU ARE GOING TO INDULGE IN A SUCCULENT BEEF STEAK, SPARERIBS OR LAMB CHOPS OCCASIONALLY, WHY NOT THOROUGHLY ENJOY THE EXPERIENCE WITH ONE OF THESE SOULFUL CREATIONS? SINCE BEEF, LAMB AND PORK ARE NATURAL CARRIERS FOR THE CHILES AND SPICES OF LATIN CUISINE, WE LET OURSELVES GO WITH THE STICKIEST, SPICIEST SPARE RIBS EVER; THICK SESAME, CELERY AND CUMIN SEED–ENCRUSTED LAMB CHOPS, AND A GRILLED STEAK STUFFED WITH WHOLE CHILES AND GARLIC THAT WILL KNOCK YOUR SOCKS OFF.

TAMPICO CALVES' LIVER
Serves 2

2 tablespoons olive oil

1 onion, julienned

1/2 teaspoon salt

5 garlic cloves, slivered

1/2 jalapeño chile, stemmed, seeded and julienned

2 Roma tomatoes, cored, seeded and julienned

12 green olives, pitted and julienned

3 tablespoons red wine vinegar

3/4 cup chicken stock

1 tablespoon cold unsalted butter

1 tablespoon vegetable oil

2 (6-ounce) slices calves' liver, about 1/2 inch thick

SINCE OUR LOS ANGELES RESTAURANTS ARE KNOWN FOR SERVING SOME OF THE BEST VARIETY CUTS IN TOWN, WE OWED IT TO OUR FANS TO COME UP WITH SOMETHING DIFFERENT FOR THE BORDER GRILL. HERE IS OUR TAKE ON MEXICAN LIVER, SAUTÉED WITH JALAPEÑOS, GARLIC AND JUST THE RIGHT DROP OF VINEGAR.

Heat the olive oil in a large skillet over medium-high heat. Sauté the onions with the salt until well caramelized, 8 to 10 minutes. Add the garlic and sauté 2 to 3 minutes longer to soften. Add the jalapeño, tomatoes, olives and vinegar. Bring to a boil. Pour in the chicken stock, bring back to a boil and simmer 10 minutes. Break the butter into a few pieces and whisk into the sauce. Remove from the heat.

Heat the vegetable oil in a large skillet over high heat. Cook the liver 3 minutes per side. Then pour in the sauce, bring to a boil and remove from the heat. Serve immediately.

GRILLED MARINATED SKIRT STEAK

Serves 6

¾ cup cumin seeds

6 jalapeño chiles, stemmed, cut in half and seeded if desired

4 garlic cloves, peeled

2 tablespoons cracked black pepper

½ cup freshly squeezed lime juice

3 bunches cilantro, stems and leaves

1½ cups olive oil

2 teaspoons salt

3 pounds skirt steak, trimmed of excess fat and cut into 6 serving pieces

1 recipe Avocado Corn Relish, page 45

warm Flour Tortillas, page 134, for serving

SKIRT IS A THIN, INEXPENSIVE CUT OF BEEF SIMILAR TO FLANK BUT WITH BETTER FLAVOR AND TEXTURE. THIS STRONG CUMIN-SCENTED MARINADE IS A GOOD FOIL FOR ITS STRONG BEEF FLAVOR. SERVE WITH MOROS (SEE PAGE 51), A CHOPPED TOMATO SALAD AND AVOCADO CORN RELISH FOR A GREAT SUMMER BARBECUE.

Lightly toast the cumin seeds in a dry medium skillet over low heat just until their aroma is released, about 5 minutes. Transfer seeds to a blender.

Add the jalapeños, garlic, black pepper, salt and lime juice and puree until the cumin seeds are finely ground. Then add the cilantro, olive oil and salt and puree until smooth.

Cut the steak into 6 serving pieces. Generously brush the meat all over with the cumin seed marinade and roll each piece up into a cylinder. Arrange the rolled steaks in a shallow pan and pour on the remaining marinade. Cover and marinate in the refrigerator 24 to 48 hours.

About 30 minutes before cooking, remove the meat from the refrigerator. Unroll the steaks and place on a platter.

Heat the grill or broiler to very hot.

Cook the steaks just until seared on both sides, 3 to 4 minutes per side for medium rare. (Or panfry in a hot cast-iron skillet lightly coated with oil.) Transfer to a cutting board and slice across the grain into diagonal strips. (Tough cuts like this and flank should always be sliced across the grain so that no one bite will contain too much muscle.) Serve hot with avocado corn relish and warm flour tortillas.

MEXICAN BRISKET OF BEEF

Serves 6

3½ pounds beef brisket

1 tablespoon coarse salt

2 teaspoons freshly ground black pepper

flour for dredging

½ cup vegetable oil

3 large carrots, peeled and cut into 2-inch lengths

2 medium onions, chopped

10 garlic cloves, peeled

3 dried chipotle or morita chiles

2 tablespoons tomato paste

1 tablespoon dried oregano

2 quarts chicken stock or water

5 bay leaves

salt to taste

1 cup Pickled Red Onions (page 46), for garnish

4 scallions, white and light green parts, thinly sliced on the diagonal, for garnish

WE GOT SUCH GOOD FEEDBACK ON OUR BRISKET RECIPE IN *CITY CUISINE*, WE JUST COULDN'T RESIST ADAPTING IT WITH MEXICAN FLAVORS. THE CHIPOTLES ADD A PLEASANT MOUTH-TINGLING SENSATION THAT IS NOT AT ALL OVERPOWERING. SERVE WITH SMASHED POTATOES (PAGE 55) FOR A SPECIAL SUNDAY SUPPER.

Preheat the oven to 325°F.

Sprinkle the brisket with the coarse salt and pepper. Dredge in flour to coat and shake off any excess.

Heat the oil in a large Dutch oven over high heat. Sear the meat until browned on all sides, and remove. Reduce the heat to moderate and add the carrots and onions. Cook, stirring occasionally, until golden brown, 8 to 10 minutes. Add the garlic and sauté 2 minutes longer. Return the meat to the pan along with all the remaining ingredients except the salt and garnishes. Bring to a boil, cover the pot and transfer to the oven. Bake for 2¼ hours, or until the meat slips off a fork when pierced.

Lift out the brisket and place on a cutting board. Cover with a damp towel. Pour the broth with vegetables into a tall container and skim off the layer of fat that rises. Remove and discard the bay leaves and chiles. Pour the broth and vegetables into a blender or a food processor fitted with the metal blade. Puree until smooth, add salt to taste and strain. Reheat the sauce.

Slice the brisket against the grain and arrange on a platter. Pour the warm sauce over it, sprinkle with pickled onions and sliced scallions and serve.

GAUCHO STUFFED RIB EYE STEAK

Serves 4

¼ cup olive oil

8 to 12 small serrano chiles, stemmed, seeded if desired

16 garlic cloves, peeled

4 (10 to 12-ounce) rib eye steaks, at least 1 inch thick

salt and freshly ground black pepper

1 recipe Green Chile Paste, page 43

THESE SUCCULENT THICK STEAKS STUFFED WITH WHOLE CHILES AND GARLIC CLOVES ARE FOR UNABASHED MEAT-AND-CHILE LOVERS ONLY. THE EASY GREEN CHILE PASTE, WHICH CAN BE SERVED ON THE SIDE IF YOU ARE UN-SURE HOW YOUR GUESTS RELATE TO CHILES, IS ALSO A NATURAL FOIL FOR RICH FOODS LIKE PORK CARNITAS AND QUESADILLAS.

If grilling, preheat the grill.

Heat the olive oil in a small saucepan over moderate heat until hot. Add the serranos and sauté until the skins start to brown and the chiles soften, about 2 minutes. Remove with a slotted spoon and drain on paper towels. Add the garlic and cook over low heat until soft and lightly browned, 4 to 6 minutes. Transfer to paper towels and let cool.

With a paring knife, make five or six 1-inch horizontal slits along the edge of each steak. Stuff each slit with either a garlic clove or chile. Season all over with salt and pepper.

Grill the steaks, or sauté in a lightly oiled cast-iron pan over high heat, 2 to 3 minutes per side for medium rare. Coat serving plates with the green chile paste and top each with a steak. Serve hot.

SABANA

Serves 2

⅓ cup dried black beans, washed and picked over

2 cups water

3 slices bacon, cut into ½-inch-wide strips

½ onion, diced

salt and freshly ground black pepper

2 (8-ounce) beef tenderloin fillets

2 teaspoons vegetable oil

1 tablespoon unsalted butter

1 bunch scallions, white and light green parts, thinly sliced on the diaganal

3 red jalapeño chiles, stemmed, seeded and julienned

juice of 1 lime

IN THIS TRADITIONAL DISH, TENDERLOINS OF BEEF ARE POUNDED PAPER-THIN, LIKE A SHEET, OR *SABANA*. THEY ARE THEN BRIEFLY SEARED AND THEN LAID ACROSS A LAYER OF MOIST BLACK BEANS AND TOPPED WITH ONIONS AND PEPPERS. THE MEAT IS SO TENDER YOU COULD EAT IT WITH A SPOON. IT IS A GREAT ELEGANT MEAL FOR A SMALL DINNER PARTY.

Place the beans and water in a medium saucepan. Bring to a boil, reduce to a simmer and cook, covered, until soft throughout, about 1 hour and 15 minutes. Remove from the heat.

Fry the bacon in a medium skillet over low heat until golden. Spoon off excess fat. Add the onion and sauté until lightly golden. Add the beans with their liquid, ½ teaspoon salt and ½ teaspoon pepper and cook 2 minutes longer. The mixture should remain thin and soupy. Keep warm. This may be prepared a day or 2 in advance and refrigerated. Reheat before serving.

To flatten the steaks, coat four 15 × 12-inch sheets of plastic or parchment paper with ½ teaspoon of the oil each. Sandwich each tenderloin, with the grain running vertically, between 2 sheets (with the oiled side facing the meat). Flatten each one with the flat side of a heavy cleaver or mallet, using steady even sweeping strokes from the center out as you would roll pie dough, until the steak is a thin oval of about 14 × 10 inches. (It takes about 5 minutes per steak.)

Preheat a lightly oiled very large nonstick skillet or cast-iron pan.

Peel the paper off the steaks and season all over with salt and pepper. Sear, one at a time, in the hot pan 30 to 40 seconds per side. Coat each of two large serving plates (platters would be great) with the warm bean mixture. Top each with a hot steak.

Prepare the garnish by melting the butter in a small hot skillet over medium-high heat. Sauté the scallions and jalapeños with salt and pepper to taste and the lime juice for 1 minute. Sprinkle over the steaks. Serve immediately.

Seeded Lamb Chops with Tamarind

Serves 4

12 ounces tamarind pods (see page 9), peeled

1 tablespoon unsalted butter

6 shallots, diced

1 teaspoon salt, plus more to taste

½ teaspoon freshly ground black pepper

3 large garlic cloves, minced

½ cup chicken stock

1 tablespoon Worcestershire sauce

½ teaspoon cayenne pepper

1½ tablespoons honey

1½ tablespoons cracked black pepper

3 tablespoons sesame seeds

3 tablespoons cumin seeds

1 tablespoon celery seeds

8 (4-ounce) lamb chops

¾ cup vegetable oil

THIS MIXED SEED CRUST WAS SUGGESTED BY OUR FRIEND GREG DUDA BECAUSE THE TYPICAL CRUST OF ONLY CRACKED BLACK PEPPERCORNS IS TOO OVERPOWERING FOR MANY TASTES. THE SAME TREATMENT, INCLUDING THE SOUR TAMARIND SAUCE, WOULD BE WONDERFUL WITH BEEF STEAKS. (IF YOU NEED TO COOK THE CHOPS IN BATCHES, BE SURE TO WIPE OUT THE PAN IN BETWEEN TO REMOVE ANY BURNT SEEDS.)

Place the tamarind in a large saucepan and pour in enough water to cover by 1 inch. Cook over medium-low heat, covered, until soft, about 30 minutes. Mash and then push through a strainer, discarding the seeds and strings. Reserve the pulp.

Melt the butter in a saucepan over medium-high heat. Sauté the shallots with the salt and ground pepper until golden brown. Add the garlic and cook 2 minutes longer. Add the chicken stock and tamarind pulp. Bring to a boil, reduce to a simmer and cook 10 minutes. Stir in the Worcestershire, cayenne and honey. Remove from the heat and keep warm.

Preheat the oven to 350°F.

Mix together the cracked pepper and sesame, cumin and celery seeds in a small shallow bowl. Season the chops all over with salt. Firmly press each into the seed mixture to coat all over. Set aside.

In a large, preferably cast-iron, skillet that comfortably holds all 8 chops, heat the oil to very hot but not smoking. Cook the chops in the bubbling oil until the seeds are golden, about 2 minutes per side. (Do not worry about a few seeds slipping off.) Transfer to a baking dish and bake 2 minutes for medium rare.

To serve, coat each of 4 plates with the tamarind sauce. Top with 2 lamb chops each and serve.

SPICY BABY BACK RIBS

Serves 4

¼ cup paprika

¼ cup ground ancho chiles or chile powder

¼ cup cumin

2 tablespoons salt

4½ pounds pork baby back ribs

HONEY GLAZE

¼ cup chopped garlic (about 15 cloves)

3 large jalapeño chiles, stemmed, seeded if desired

1 tablespoon ground cumin

3 tablespoons Tabasco

1 cup freshly squeezed lime juice

1 teaspoon salt

1 cup honey

OUR METHOD FOR TENDERIZING RIBS AND OTHER TOUGH CUTS INVOLVES TWO TECHNIQUES. FIRST THE RIBS ARE BAKED IN A SMALL AMOUNT OF WATER TO STEAM AND SOFTEN SO THE FLAVORS PENETRATE. THEN THEY ARE BRIEFLY CRISPED ON THE GRILL BEFORE SERVING. THE RESULTS ARE TENDER, SWEET, SPICY, WONDERFULLY STICKY RIBS.

Combine the paprika, chile powder, cumin and salt in a small bowl. Pat the spice mixture all over the ribs. Cover with plastic wrap and refrigerate 2 to 4 hours or overnight.

Preheat the oven to 350°F.

Place the ribs in a single layer in a baking pan and pour in water to a depth of about ¼ inch. Bake, uncovered, 45 minutes. Cover with foil and return to the oven for an additional 30 minutes.

Meanwhile, make the honey glaze: Combine the garlic, jalapeños, cumin, Tabasco, lime juice and salt in a food processor or blender and puree. Pour into a small saucepan and stir in the honey. Cook over low heat, stirring constantly and being careful not to burn, 20 minutes.

Turn the oven heat up to 450°F or heat the grill.

If finishing the ribs in the oven, brush generously with the honey glaze and bake another 10 minutes per side, basting with the honey glaze every 5 minutes. To grill, generously glaze the ribs and grill 5 minutes per side, frequently brushing with additional glaze. Cut the ribs apart and serve hot.

PORK STEAKS ADOBO

Serves 4

4 (8-ounce) pork sirloin, butt or shoulder steaks or chops

2½ cups Adobo, page 42

salt and freshly ground black pepper

AS THE MEAT COOKS, THE SUGARS FROM THE MARINADE CARAMELIZE AND CREATE A SLIGHTLY CRISP, CHARRED CRUST. THESE EASY STEAKS WOULD MAKE A NICE SUMMER BARBECUE WITH GRILLED CORN OR WITH A SIDE DISH OF AVOCADO CORN RELISH (PAGE 45).

Combine the steaks with the adobo in a shallow nonreactive roasting pan and let marinate at room temperature 2 to 4 hours or overnight in the refrigerator.

Preheat the grill or broiler.

Lift the meat from the marinade, shaking off the excess, and season all over with salt and pepper. Cook over moderate heat, or 4 inches from the broiler unit, turning frequently and brushing several times with the marinade during the last few minutes, until slightly charred, about 10 minutes.

PICKLED PORK TENDERLOIN

Serves 4

BRINE

2 quarts water

¼ cup sugar

3 tablespoons salt

1 tablespoon cumin seeds

1 tablespoon black peppercorns, cracked

6 bay leaves

½ bunch thyme

½ bunch oregano

2 pork tenderloins

¼ cup vegetable oil

1 recipe Orange Cilantro Salsa, page 197

MARINATING PORK TENDERLOIN IN A SPICY PICKLING BRINE GIVES EXTRAORDINARY TEXTURE AND FLAVOR TO AN ORDINARILY DULL CUT OF MEAT. WE LIKE TO SHOWCASE IT SIMPLY ALONGSIDE A BED OF BLACK BEANS, WITH A DOLLOP OF ORANGE CILANTRO SALSA TO KEEP THINGS MOIST AND INTERESTING.

Bring the water to a boil in a large saucepan. Add the remaining brine ingredients and set aside to cool. Place the tenderloins in the brine, cover and refrigerate 8 hours or overnight.

To cook, preheat the oven to 425°F.

Heat the oil in an ovenproof skillet over high heat. Sear the tenderloins all over. Then transfer to the oven and bake for 8 to 10 minutes. Transfer to a cutting board. Cut the meat into ¼-inch diagonal slices across the grain and fan on serving plates. Top with the orange salsa and serve.

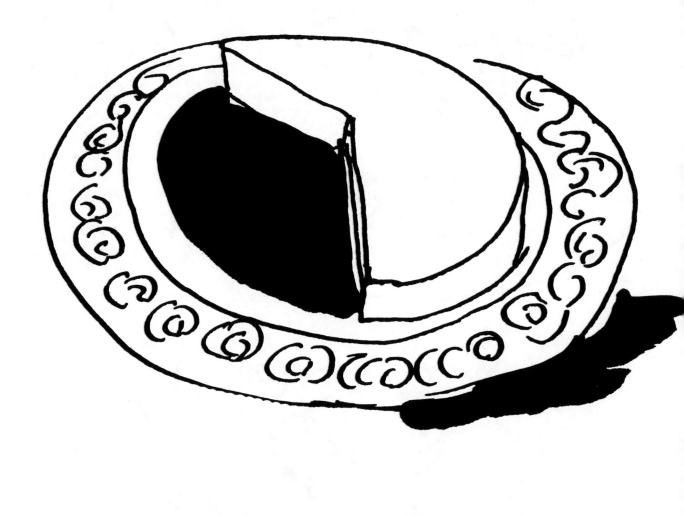

Desserts

We veered quite a bit from the traditional Mexican menu in designing the dessert selections for the Border Grill. After developing a foolproof recipe for flan, the scrumptious Mexican dessert, we started playing with native ingredients like chocolate, coconut, pineapple, guava and assorted nuts and spices and took them in the direction of the kind of all-American cakes, cookies, pies, puddings and ice creams we (and our customers) love best.

FLANS

E GGS

PLAIN FLAN

Serves 8 to 10

6 large eggs

6 large egg yolks

½ cup sugar

2 teaspoons vanilla extract

2 cups half-and-half

1 recipe Homemade Condensed Milk, page 231

1 vanilla bean

MARY SUE'S OBSESSION WITH CUSTARD MAKING ENJOYS FULL EXPRESSION IN THESE CAREFULLY REFINED RECIPES. IN PURSUIT OF THE PERFECT FLAN SINCE WE STARTED SERVING THEM IN 1985, SHE HAS A FEW POINTERS TO PASS ALONG: IT IS ALWAYS BETTER TO SLIGHTLY UNDERCOOK RATHER THAN OVERCOOK A FLAN. ADJUST YOUR OVEN TEMPERATURE DOWNWARDS IF IT RUNS TOO HOT. BE SURE TO SURROUND THE DISH WITH A GENEROUS WATER BATH. AND TEST FOR DONENESS BY LOOKING FOR A SLIGHT SHIMMER RATHER THAN BIG WAVES WHEN THE CENTER IS PRESSED. (AIR BUBBLES IN THE FINISHED CUSTARD MEAN IT HAS BEEN OVERCOOKED.) WHEN IT COMES TO FLANS, PRACTICE MAKES PERFECT.

Preheat the oven to 325°F.

In a large mixing bowl, gently whisk together the eggs, egg yolks, sugar, vanilla extract and half-and-half, without incorporating air.

Pour the condensed milk into a saucepan. Split the vanilla bean lengthwise and, using the tip of a paring knife, scrape the black seeds into the milk. Add the bean and bring to a boil.

Eggs

Gradually pour the hot milk into the egg mixture, whisking constantly. Pass through a strainer into the caramel-coated cake pan. Place inside a large roasting pan and pour in hot tap water until it rises halfway up the sides of the flan.

Bake 1 hour to 1 hour and 10 minutes, until the center just feels firm when pressed. Set aside to cool in the pan of water. Then remove from the water bath, cover with plastic wrap and refrigerate 4 to 6 hours or overnight.

To serve, run a knife along the inside edge of the pan and gently press the center of the bottom to loosen. Cover with a platter, invert and lift off the pan. Excess caramel can be drained from the cake pan and added to the reserved caramel sauce. Cut in wedges and serve topped with cold caramel sauce.

CARAMEL

2 cups sugar

1¼ cups water

Have ready a 9-inch round cake pan. Combine the sugar and ½ cup of the water in a medium saucepan. Use a pastry brush dipped in cold water to wash down any sugar granules from the pot's sides. Cook over moderate heat, swirling the pan occasionally, until the color is dark brown and the mixture has the distinctive fragrance of caramel, 10 to 15 minutes. Pour enough of the caramel into a 9-inch round cake pan to coat the bottom and sides. Swirl to coat evenly.

Slowly and carefully add the remaining ¾ cup water to the caramel in the saucepan. Bring to a boil and cook over moderate heat until the caramel dissolves, about 5 minutes. Occasionally stir and brush down the sides with the pastry brush dipped in cold water to prevent crystallization. Set this caramel sauce aside to cool and then chill until serving time.

Chocolate Espresso Flan

Serves 8

1 recipe Caramel, page 227

1¾ cups Homemade Condensed Milk,
page 231

2 ounces good-quality semisweet
chocolate, chopped

¼ cup heavy cream

6 large eggs

7 large egg yolks

2 cups half-and-half

¾ cup packed brown sugar

½ cup brewed espresso

¼ cup Kahlúa or other coffee liqueur

BROWN SUGAR AND COFFEE UNDERLINE THE WONDERFUL RICH FLAVOR OF CHOCOLATE—A NATIVE MEXICAN INGREDIENT.

Prepare the caramel and coat a 9-inch round cake pan, reserving the extra sauce in the refrigerator as directed on page 227.

Preheat the oven to 350°F.

Combine the condensed milk, chocolate and heavy cream in a heatproof medium mixing bowl. Set over simmering water and cook, stirring occasionally, until the chocolate is melted and smooth. Remove from heat.

Combine the remaining ingredients in a large mixing bowl and beat until well blended. Pour in the melted chocolate mixture. Stir to combine and pass through a fine strainer into the caramel-coated cake pan.

Place inside a large roasting pan and pour in hot tap water until it rises halfway up the sides of the flan. Bake about 1 hour, until the center just feels firm when pressed. Remove from the hot water and let cool to room temperature. Cover with plastic wrap and refrigerate overnight.

To serve, run a knife along the inside edge of the pan to loosen the flan and invert onto a serving tray. Pour off any excess caramel and serve with the reserved cold caramel sauce.

FLAN

RED YAM FLAN

Serves 8 to 10

1 large yam or sweet potato (about 18 ounces) or 1 cup canned pureed yams or sweet potatoes

vegetable oil

1 recipe Caramel, page 227

¾ cup packed brown sugar

1 tablespoon ground cinnamon

1½ teaspoons allspice

1½ teaspoons ground cloves

2 cups half-and-half

2 cups Homemade Condensed Milk, page 231

6 large eggs

6 large egg yolks

1½ teaspoons vanilla extract

3 tablespoons dark rum

THIS VELVETY CUSTARD FLAVORED WITH TYPICAL PUMPKIN PIE SPICES WOULD BE NICE ON A MEXICAN BUFFET OR AFTER A HOLIDAY DINNER.

Preheat the oven to 400°F if using a fresh yam. Rub the yam with vegetable oil, place on a baking tray and bake 45 minutes to 1 hour, until a knife easily pierces the potato at its thickest part. Set aside until cool enough to handle, then peel and mash with a fork. (The mashed potato should measure about 1 cup.)

Reduce the oven temperature to 325°F (or preheat).

Prepare the caramel and coat a 9-inch round cake pan, reserving the extra sauce in the refrigerator as directed on page 227.

Combine all of the remaining ingredients with the mashed or pureed yams in a large bowl and thoroughly mix. Pass through a strainer, pressing with a spatula, into the coated cake pan.

Place the cake pan inside a larger roasting pan and fill with hot tap water to come halfway up the sides of the smaller pan. Bake 1 hour and 10 minutes to 1 hour and 20 minutes, or until the center just feels firm when pressed. Set aside to cool in the water bath. Remove from the water bath, cover with plastic wrap and refrigerate 4 to 6 hours or overnight.

To serve, run a knife along the inside edge of the pan and gently press the center of the bottom to loosen. Cover with a platter, invert and remove the pan. Excess caramel can be drained from the pan and added to the reserved caramel sauce. Cut in wedges and serve topped with cold caramel sauce.

COCONUT FLAN

Serves 8 to 10

1 recipe Caramel, page 227

6 large eggs

6 large egg yolks

½ cup sugar

2 cups half-and-half

¾ cup canned unsweetened coconut milk

1 teaspoon vanilla extract

2 cups Homemade Condensed Milk, page 231

1 cup grated sweetened coconut

THIS COMBINATION OF COCONUT, CARAMEL AND SMOOTH RICH CUSTARD IS HEAVEN FOR COCONUT LOVERS.

Prepare the caramel and coat a 9-inch cake pan, reserving the extra sauce in the refrigerator as directed on page 227.

Preheat the oven to 325°F.

Combine the eggs, egg yolks, sugar, half-and-half, coconut milk and vanilla extract in a large mixing bowl. Gently whisk, being careful not to incorporate air.

Pour the condensed milk into a saucepan and bring to a boil.

Gradually pour the hot milk into the egg mixture, whisking constantly. Pass through a strainer into the caramel-coated cake pan. Sprinkle the grated coconut evenly over the top.

Place inside a large roasting pan and pour in hot tap water until it rises halfway up the sides of the flan. Bake about 1 hour or until the center just firm feels when pressed. Set aside to cool in the roasting pan. Remove from the water bath, cover with plastic wrap and refrigerate 4 to 6 hours or overnight.

To serve, run a knife along inside edge of the pan and gently press the center of the bottom to loosen. Cover with a platter, invert and remove the pan. Excess caramel can be drained from the pan and added to the reserved caramel sauce. Cut in wedges and serve topped with cold caramel sauce.

HOMEMADE CONDENSED MILK

Makes 3 cups

6 cups nonfat milk

5 tablespoons sugar

WE STARTED MAKING OUR OWN CONDENSED MILK AS A RE-ACTION TO THE OVERLY SWEETENED CANNED PRODUCT. AN ADDED BONUS IS THAT YOU CAN USE NONFAT MILK.

Pour the milk into a medium heavy saucepan and bring to a boil. Reduce to a simmer and cook 45 minutes, stirring occasionally. Stir in the sugar and continue simmering 10 to 15 minutes or until reduced to 3 cups. Strain. Homemade condensed milk can be refrigerated up to a week.

COOKIES

DEEP CHOCOLATE SCOOTERS

Makes about 26 cookies

½ cup raisins

2 tablespoons brandy

2 ounces unsweetened chocolate, coarsely chopped

4 ounces bittersweet chocolate, coarsely chopped

3 tablespoons unsalted butter

¼ cup all-purpose flour

¼ teaspoon baking powder

¼ teaspoon salt

2 large eggs

¾ cup sugar

1 teaspoon vanilla extract

2¼ teaspoons finely ground espresso beans

⅔ cup semisweet chocolate chips

THESE TENDER DARK CHOCOLATE COOKIES PUNCTUATED BY BITS OF RAISIN WERE TAUGHT TO US BY A COOK NAMED SCOOTER. THE TRICK TO WORKING WITH SUCH A THIN, FRAGILE DOUGH IS NOT TO OVERCOOK, TO LET THE COOKIES SET WELL ON THE SHEETS BEFORE LIFTING AND NOT TO STACK UNTIL FULLY COOLED.

Preheat the oven to 350°F. Line cookie sheets with parchment paper.

Combine the raisins and brandy in a small saucepan and warm over low heat. Set aside to cool.

Combine the unsweetened and bittersweet chocolates with the butter in a heavy saucepan and place over low heat, stirring occasionally, until melted and smooth. Set aside to cool.

Stir together the flour, baking powder and salt in a bowl and set aside.

Beat the eggs and sugar until pale and thick, about 5 minutes. Beat in the vanilla and espresso.

Pour in the melted chocolate and fold to combine. Then fold in the dry ingredients. Stir in the chocolate chips and raisins. The dough will be quite loose.

Spoon about a tablespoon of batter for each cookie onto the lined cookie sheets. Bake 6 to 8 minutes, until the tops are cracked and shiny and the cookies slightly puffed. Let cool on the cookie sheet and then transfer to racks.

PAJAS

Makes 20 to 24 cookies

1 cup pecan halves

1 tablespoon unsalted butter, melted

2½ cups sweetened shredded coconut

½ cup chopped dried apricots

½ cup chopped semisweet chocolate or chocolate morsels

7 ounces canned sweetened condensed milk

WE LOVE THE WAY THE TARTNESS OF DRIED APRICOTS BALANCES THE RICH, SWEET CHOCOLATE AND COCONUT IN THESE CHEWY HAYSTACK COOKIES—REMINISCENT OF THE STICKY COCONUT CANDIES OFTEN FOUND IN MEXICO CITY'S SWEET SHOPS. THEY ARE A GOOD CHOICE FOR LAST-MINUTE ENTERTAINING SINCE ALL THE MIXING CAN BE DONE BY HAND IN ABOUT FIVE MINUTES.

Preheat the oven to 325°F. Line a cookie sheet with parchment paper, or use a nonstick pan.

Toss the pecans in the melted butter to evenly coat. Spread the nuts on an ungreased baking sheet and bake 10 to 15 minutes, or until golden and aromatic. Set aside to cool, and then roughly chop.

Place the chopped pecans and the remaining ingredients in a bowl and mix with a wooden spoon until evenly moistened.

Spoon about 2 tablespoons of batter for each cookie onto the lined cookie sheet and gently flatten to circles of about 2¼ inches in diameter. (These cookies do not spread.) Bake 10 minutes or until the coconut turns very pale golden, being careful not to overbrown. Transfer to racks to cool.

BORDER SUGAR COOKIES

Makes about 24 cookies

8 ounces (2 sticks) unsalted butter, softened

½ cup sugar

¾ teaspoon salt

1½ teaspoons vanilla extract

½ cup chopped pecans

½ cup crushed potato chips

2 cups unbleached all-purpose flour

sugar for dipping

4 ounces semisweet chocolate, for garnish (optional)

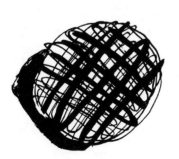

MARY SUE'S MOTHER, RUTH, CAME UP WITH THE SECRET IN-GREDIENT—POTATO CHIPS—THAT GIVES THESE CRUMBLY SUGAR COOKIES THEIR IRRESISTIBLE CRUNCH. IT IS ONLY A SMALL AMOUNT, BUT WHAT A TERRIFIC DIFFERENCE IT MAKES. JUST PLACE A FEW HANDFULS IN A BAG AND CRUSH WITH A ROLLING PIN OR THE PALMS OF YOUR HAND. THESE SUGAR COOKIES STAY FRESH FOR A COUPLE OF WEEKS STORED IN AN AIRTIGHT TIN.

Preheat the oven to 350°F. Line a cookie sheet with parchment paper.

Cream together the butter and sugar until light and fluffy. Beat in the salt and vanilla. Then add the pecans and potato chips and mix well. With a wooden spoon, stir in the flour just until it disappears.

Roll the batter into balls about the size of a large walnut and place on the parchment-lined cookie sheet, allowing plenty of room for spreading. Coat the bottom of a heavy glass with butter and then dip in sugar. Press and twist to flatten each ball into a 3-inch circle. Bake 8 to 10 minutes or until the edges turn lightly golden brown. Transfer to racks to cool.

For optional garnish, melt the chocolate in a bowl over a pot of simmering water. Let cool slightly. When cool enough to handle, dip your fingertips, or the tines of a fork, in the chocolate and drizzle over the cookies. Refrigerate to set.

Coconut Jam Fills

Makes about 24 cookies

1¾ cup grated sweetened coconut

1½ cups all-purpose flour

1 teaspoon baking soda

1 teaspoon salt

1½ cups rolled oats

12 tablespoons (1½ sticks) unsalted butter, softened

¾ cup packed brown sugar

1 large egg

½ teaspoon vanilla extract

⅔ cup guava or other jam

THESE CRUMBLY, NOT-TOO-SWEET THUMBPRINT COOKIES ARE A GOOD WHOLESOME CHILDREN'S SNACK. THEY ALSO MAKE A NICE CHRISTMAS COOKIE.

Preheat the oven to 325°F. Line a cookie sheet with parchment paper.

Place the grated coconut in a shallow bowl and set aside.

Combine the flour, baking soda, salt and oats in a large mixing bowl.

In another bowl, cream together the butter and brown sugar until light and fluffy. Then beat in the egg and vanilla. Add the flour mixture and mix just until combined.

To shape cookies, roll the batter between your hands to form balls the size of a large walnut. Roll in the grated coconut to coat, then place on the cookie sheet and flatten to 2-inch circles with the palm of your hand. With your thumb, make a depression in the center of each and fill with a generous teaspoonful of jam. Bake 20 to 25 minutes, until lightly browned. Transfer to racks to cool.

CAKES

OAXACAN CHOCOLATE MOCHA CAKE

Serves 8 to 10

1 pound bittersweet chocolate, chopped, plus 3 ounces, melted

8 ounces (2 sticks) unsalted butter

6 large eggs

2 tablespoons finely ground espresso beans

2 cups pecan halves

2 cups Crema, page 249, or crème fraîche

½ cup confectioners' sugar

1 teaspoon vanilla extract

WHAT MAKES THIS MEXICAN FLOURLESS CHOCOLATE CAKE SUCH A STANDOUT IS THE CONTRAST BETWEEN THE DENSE BOTTOM LAYER OF THICK DARK CHOCOLATE AND THE EQUALLY THICK TOP LAYER OF SLIGHTLY TART CRÈME FRAÎCHE. SUSAN, AN INVETERATE CHOCOHOLIC, LIKES TO EAT AT LEAST ONE SERVING A DAY TO KEEP HER METABOLISM IN BALANCE.

Preheat the oven to 425°F. Line a 9-inch round cake pan with parchment paper.

Combine the chopped chocolate and butter in a large heatproof mixing bowl over simmering water, or the top of a double boiler, and stir frequently until melted. Remove from the heat.

Place the eggs in a mixing bowl over warm tap water until luke-warm. Then beat with an electric mixer until light in color and tripled in volume, about 3 minutes at medium speed and then at high speed for 5 minutes longer.

Add half the beaten eggs and the ground espresso beans to the chocolate mixture and fold in. Then add the remaining eggs and gently fold in until just a few streaks remain. Do not overmix.

Pour into the cake pan and place in a roasting pan. Fill the roasting pan with boiling water to come halfway up the cake pan, transfer to the oven and bake for 5 minutes. Cover the cake pan with aluminum foil and bake—still in its water bath—an additional 10 minutes. Set aside to cool on rack 45 minutes, then refrigerate at least 6 hours or overnight.

Reduce the oven temperature to 350°F.

Spread the pecan halves on a baking sheet and toast in the oven until golden, 10 to 15 minutes. Set aside to cool.

To remove the cake from the pan, place the pan over a low burner for a moment or two. Run a sharp knife around the inside edge to loosen the cake and invert onto a platter.

Whisk the crema or crème fraîche with the sugar and vanilla until peaks form. Pile the stiff cream on the chocolate cake. Then, using a spatula, spread it out to the edges to make a thick even layer of cream over the top, being careful not to drip the white cream onto the sides of the cake. Refrigerate for 10 minutes to set. Then arrange the pecan halves on top of the cream to form a circle around the outside edge. Dip your fingertips or a fork into the melted chocolate and drizzle over the center in a free-form pattern. Refrigerate until serving time. The finished cake can be held overnight.

Rum Walnut Cake

Serves 8 to 10

1 cup walnut halves

2 cups raisins

¾ cup dark rum

¼ cup water

1½ cups walnut pieces, roughly chopped

¼ cup honey

¼ cup sour cream

4 cups all-purpose flour

2½ teaspoons baking powder

1½ teaspoons baking soda

10 ounces (2½ sticks) unsalted butter, softened

1½ cups packed brown sugar

2 teaspoons vanilla extract

1 teaspoon salt

5 large eggs

GLAZE

4 tablespoons unsalted butter

½ cup sugar

2 tablespoons water

¼ cup rum

THIS IS AN ADAPTATION OF MARY SUE'S MOTHER'S CLASSIC SOUR CREAM COFFEE CAKE, WITH A LIBERAL DOSE OF RUM-SOAKED RAISINS AND TOASTED NUTS. IT IS A SURE HIT FOR WEEKEND BRUNCH AND AFTERNOON SNACKS.

Preheat the oven to 325°F. Generously butter a large Bundt pan. Evenly spread the walnut halves over the bottom of the pan.

Combine the raisins, ½ cup of the rum and the water in a small saucepan. Cook over low heat, shaking frequently, until all the liquid is absorbed. Set aside to cool, and then stir in the chopped walnuts. Reserve.

Combine the honey, sour cream and remaining ¼ cup rum in a small bowl and reserve.

In another bowl, stir together the flour, baking powder and soda.

With an electric mixer, cream together the butter and brown sugar until light and fluffy. Beat in the vanilla and salt. Add the eggs, one at a time, beating about a minute at medium speed after each addition.

Add the flour mixture, alternating with the sour cream/honey combination, in five parts, mixing gently between additions. (The last addition should be the liquids.) Fold in the rum-soaked raisins and nuts.

Spoon the batter evenly into the prepared pan. Poke the batter in a few places with a knife to release large air bubbles. Smooth the top with a spatula and tap on a counter twice to release air bubbles. Bake 1 to 1¼ hours, until a skewer inserted in the center comes out dry. Cool on a rack while preparing the glaze.

To make the glaze, combine the butter, sugar and water in a small saucepan. Bring to a boil and let boil 2 minutes. Remove from the heat and stir in the rum.

To glaze, poke a few deep holes in the cake with a skewer or toothpick. Brush on one-third of the glaze. Invert the cake onto a baking pan and remove the cake pan. Brush the remaining glaze over the top, sides and down the center. Let cool completely before transferring to a platter and slicing.

FRESH PINEAPPLE UPSIDE-DOWN CAKE

Serves 8

½ cup blanched whole almonds

4 tablespoons unsalted butter, melted, plus 9 tablespoons unsalted butter, softened

½ cup packed brown sugar

2 tablespoons light corn syrup

½ pineapple, peeled, cored, cut in half lengthwise and cut crosswise into ½-inch slices

1½ cups pastry flour

¾ cup granulated sugar

¾ teaspoon baking powder

¼ teaspoon baking soda

½ teaspoon salt

½ cup sour cream

3 large egg yolks

1 teaspoon vanilla extract

WHY RUIN A PERFECTLY GOOD SOUR CREAM UPSIDE-DOWN CAKE WITH CANNED PINEAPPLE, MARY SUE REASONED, WHEN SHE CAME UP WITH THIS REFRESHING ALTERNATIVE. ANOTHER GOOD SUBSTITUTE IS FROZEN SOUR CHERRIES, THAWED AND DRAINED, OR FRESH PLUMS.

Preheat the oven to 350°F.

Spread the almonds on a baking sheet and toast, shaking the pan occasionally, until lightly golden, 15 to 20 minutes. Set aside to cool. Turn the oven temperature down to 325°F.

Stir together the melted butter, brown sugar and corn syrup and evenly coat the bottom and sides of a 10-inch glass pie plate with the mixture. When the almonds are cool, arrange around the bottom rim of the pie plate, with a few in the center, gently pressing them into the brown sugar mixture. Arrange the pineapple in an even layer on top of the brown sugar mixture.

In a mixing bowl, combine the pastry flour, granulated sugar, baking powder, baking soda and salt and thoroughly mix.

In another bowl, whisk together the softened butter, sour cream, egg yolks and vanilla. Add to the dry ingredients and mix with an electric mixer at medium speed about 1½ minutes, scraping down the sides of the bowl occasionally, until thick and smooth.

Using a spatula, spread the batter evenly over the fruit, building up the outside edges so the cake will be level when baked. Bake 40 to 50 minutes, until golden brown and a tester inserted in the center comes out clean. Transfer to a rack to cool 3 to 5 minutes (no longer) and then invert onto a serving plate, repositioning the fruit as necessary.

Citrus Cheesecake

Serves 8 to 10

¹/₂ cup slivered almonds, toasted (see page 254)

2¹/₂ pounds cream cheese, softened

3 tablespoons all-purpose flour

1¹/₂ cups sugar

grated zest of 1 lemon

grated zest of 2 oranges

5 large eggs

2 large egg yolks

¹/₂ teaspoon vanilla extract

1 cup sour cream, for garnish (optional)

thinly sliced kumquats for garnish (optional)

Grated orange and lemon zest cut the richness of this very smooth, creamy cheesecake. If at all possible, do not pass up the optional garnish of sour cream and kumquats. They add an intriguing play of textures as well as an extra jolt of tartness that is just right.

Preheat the oven to 325°F. Butter a 9-inch round cake pan. Coat the bottom and sides with the toasted almonds.

In a large bowl, beat the cream cheese with an electric mixer at low speed until soft and smooth, about 1 minute. Combine the flour and sugar in another bowl and then add to the beaten cream cheese. Mix well, scraping down the sides of the bowl occasionally. Beat in the grated citrus zests. Add the eggs, egg yolks and vanilla extract. Mix thoroughly, frequently scraping down the sides of the bowl, until the batter is perfectly smooth.

Pour the batter into the prepared pan, tapping the bottom on a counter four or five times to eliminate air pockets. Place the cake pan inside a large roasting pan and pour in hot tap water until it rises halfway up the sides of the cake pan. Bake 1 hour, or until the center feels firm when pressed. Immediately remove the cake pan from the larger pan and set aside to cool on a rack. Refrigerate 4 to 6 hours or overnight.

To serve, place the pan over a low burner for about 1 minute to melt the butter. Invert onto a plate and then invert again onto a serving platter so the nuts are on the bottom. To garnish, spread the optional sour cream evenly over the top and cover the top with rows of thinly sliced kumquats.

ICE CREAMS, PUDDINGS, SORBETS AND SUNDAES

CINNAMON PECAN ICE CREAM

Makes 1 1/2 quarts

8 large egg yolks

1 cup plus 1 tablespoon packed brown sugar

2 1/2 cups milk

4 cinnamon sticks

1 teaspoon vanilla extract

1 teaspoon ground cinnamon

pinch of salt

1 1/2 cups Crema, page 249, or crème fraîche

1 1/4 cups pecan halves

CRÈME FRAÎCHE ADDS A PLEASANT SOUR NOTE TO THIS RICH TOASTED PECAN ICE CREAM.

In a large bowl, whisk together the egg yolks and brown sugar until thick and pale brown.

Combine the milk and cinnamon sticks in a saucepan and bring to a boil. Remove from the heat. Stir 1/2 cup of the milk into the egg mixture, then whisk the eggs into the pan of milk. Set aside to cool.

Pass the custard mixture through a medium strainer. Add the vanilla extract, ground cinnamon, salt and crema or crème fraîche. Whisk well and refrigerate until cold.

Preheat the oven to 350°F.

Spread the pecans on a baking sheet and toast until golden brown and fragrant, about 10 minutes. Set aside to cool and then roughly chop.

Pour the chilled custard mixture into your ice cream maker and process according to the manufacturer's instructions. Fold in the cooled toasted pecans. Store in the freezer.

MEXICAN
CINNAMON STICK

COCONUT ICE CREAM

Makes 1 1/2 quarts

1 medium coconut, hulled and peeled, milk reserved (see page 21)

1 (14-ounce) can unsweetened coconut milk

1 cup whole milk

8 large egg yolks

1 cup sugar

2 cups Crema, page 249, or crème fraîche

2 teaspoons vanilla extract

FRESH COCONUT DOESN'T NEED MUCH SUGAR TO ENHANCE ITS SWEET, PURE FLAVOR.

Combine the coconut meat and its milk in a food processor. Puree until finely chopped.

Pour the canned coconut milk and whole milk into a saucepan and bring to a boil.

Beat together the egg yolks and sugar until pale yellow and thick. Pour the hot milk mixture slowly into the eggs and whisk until combined. Stir in the crema or crème fraîche, pureed coconut and vanilla. Refrigerate until cold.

Pour the chilled custard mixture into your ice cream maker and process according to the manufacturer's instructions. Store in the freezer.

ICE CREAM

KAHLÚA CHIP ICE CREAM

Makes 1 ¹/₂ quarts

8 large egg yolks

1 cup sugar

1 quart half-and-half

1 tablespoon vanilla extract

¾ cup brewed double-strength espresso, cold

½ cup Kahlúa or other coffee liqueur

8 ounces semisweet chocolate, chopped

JUDY ZEIDLER, A WELL-KNOWN LOS ANGELES COOKBOOK AUTHOR, TAUGHT US THIS EASY TECHNIQUE FOR ADDING TINY CHOCOLATE BITS THAT DISSOLVE ON THE TONGUE TO ICE CREAM. JUST STIR MELTED CHOCOLATE INTO COMPLETELY PROCESSED ICE CREAM AND THEN PLACE IN THE FREEZER. THE COMBINATION OF CHOCOLATE AND COFFEE IS A PERENNIAL FAVORITE OF OURS.

Place a large mixing bowl in the freezer.

In another large bowl, whisk together the egg yolks and sugar until thick and pale yellow. Bring the half-and-half to a boil. Gradually pour into the egg mixture, whisking until the sugar dissolves. Let stand 5 minutes and then chill.

Stir the vanilla, cold espresso and Kahlúa into the chilled custard. Pass through a fine strainer. Pour into an ice cream maker and process according to the manufacturer's instructions. When the ice cream is nearly done, melt the chocolate over simmering water.

Transfer the frozen ice cream into the chilled bowl from the freezer. Pour in the melted chocolate, stirring and mixing vigorously with a wooden spoon. Transfer to a container and freeze until firm.

CANDIED PUMPKIN ICE CREAM SUNDAES

Serves 4

1 1/2 cups water

1 cup packed brown sugar

1 large Mexican cinnamon stick or 3 regular cinnamon sticks

1/2 pound pumpkin or acorn squash, peeled and cut into 2-inch cubes

1/4 cup heavy cream (optional)

1 1/2 to 2 pints vanilla ice cream

BRIGHT ORANGE CHUNKS OF SWEETENED PUMPKIN OR WINTER SQUASH ON TOP OF VANILLA ICE CREAM ARE A REFRESHING CHANGE FROM HOT FUDGE SUNDAES. YOU CAN MAKE THE CANDIED PUMPKIN WELL IN ADVANCE AND JUST REHEAT FOR LAST-MINUTE SPECIAL DESSERTS. CANDIED FRUITS AND VEGETABLES IN SYRUP ARE TRADITIONAL MEXICAN SWEETS.

Combine the water, brown sugar, and cinnamon in a medium saucepan. Bring to a boil and cook until the liquid has reduced by about one-quarter and a light syrup forms, about 15 minutes. Add the pumpkin or squash, reduce the heat to very low and simmer gently until the pumpkin is translucent, about 45 minutes. If preparing in advance, remove the pumpkin from the syrup with a slotted spoon and store the pumpkin and syrup separately. When ready to serve, combine the pumpkin and syrup in a small skillet and reheat over low heat.

Just before serving, stir the heavy cream into the pumpkin syrup. Spoon over the ice cream and serve.

TAMARIND SORBET

Makes 1 quart

2 cups water

¾ cup sugar

12 ounces tamarind pods (see page 9), peeled

1 cup light corn syrup

THIS TAMARIND SORBET, MARY SUE'S FAVORITE, IS CREAMY AND SUPREMELY SOUR—VERY REFRESHING AFTER A MEXICAN MEAL. THE CORN SYRUP HELPS TO KEEP THE ICE CRYSTALS FROM FORMING IN THE SORBET.

Bring the water and sugar to a boil in a small saucepan. Set aside to cool.

Place the tamarind in a saucepan and pour in enough water to cover by 1 inch. Cover and cook over low heat about 30 minutes, or until soft. Mash and then pass through a strainer into a bowl, discarding the seeds and strings. (You should have about 1 cup pulp.) Stir in the boiled sugar syrup and corn syrup. Refrigerate until cold.

Pour the chilled sorbet base into an ice cream maker and process according to the manufacturer's instructions. Store in the freezer.

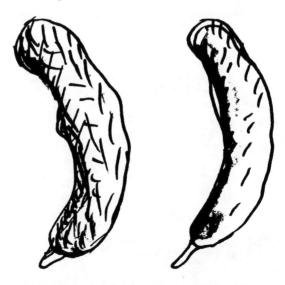

TEQUILA LIME SORBET

Makes 2¹/₂ pints

1¹/₂ cups tequila

1 cup freshly squeezed lime juice

¹/₂ cup Triple Sec

¹/₂ cup light corn syrup

2 cups Simple Syrup, recipe follows

¹/₂ cup water

2 tablespoons chia seeds, see page 18, (optional)

THIS REFRESHING CLEAR SORBET IS ONE OF THE BEST WAYS WE KNOW TO END A HEAVILY SPICED MEXICAN MEAL.

Pour the tequila into a small saucepan and bring to a boil. Cook until reduced by half (most of the alcohol will boil off). Pour into a bowl and add all of the remaining ingredients. Refrigerate until cold.

Pour the chilled mixture into an ice cream maker and process according to the manufacturer's instructions. Store in the freezer.

SIMPLE SYRUP

Makes 2 cups

1¹/₄ cups sugar

1¹/₄ cups water

Combine the sugar and water in a saucepan and bring to a boil, stirring until the sugar dissolves. Let cool.

CAPIROTADA

Serves 8 to 10

8 tablespoons (1 stick) unsalted butter

½ loaf French bread or baguette, with crust, cut into small cubes

1 pound brown sugar

1½ cups water

1½ teaspoons ground cinnamon

2 large Granny Smith apples, peeled, cored and chopped

1 cup walnuts, chopped

½ pound cream cheese, chilled and chopped

Crema, page 249, or heavy cream for garnish

MEXICAN BREAD PUDDING IS A RICH, UNFUSSY PUDDING THAT CAN BE SCOOPED OUT AND SERVED IN COZY BOWLS ALONG WITH ITS TRADITIONAL DOLLOP OF FRESH CREAM. IT IS ONE OF THE MOST POPULAR DESSERTS AT THE RESTAURANT AND AMAZINGLY ADDICTIVE, EVEN FOR AVOWED NON-BREAD PUDDING PEOPLE.

Preheat the oven to 350°F. Butter a 13 × 9-inch glass casserole or lasagna pan.

Melt the butter in a medium saucepan, add the bread cubes and stir to coat evenly. Spread the cubes on a baking sheet and bake 15 minutes or until lightly brown and crisp. Remove the bread and turn the oven temperature up to 400°F.

Combine the sugar and water in a saucepan and bring to a boil. Remove from the heat. Stir in the cinnamon and set aside.

In a large mixing bowl, combine the chopped apples, walnuts, cream cheese and toasted bread cubes. Drizzle with the reserved sugar syrup and mix to evenly distribute. Transfer the mixture to the prepared pan.

Bake, uncovered, stirring occasionally, for 15 minutes. Then bake an additional 5 minutes, without stirring, until the top is golden brown and crusty and the liquid is almost gone. Serve warm with pitchers of crema or heavy cream for adding at the table.

CREMA

Makes 2 cups

2 cups heavy cream

¼ cup buttermilk

Whisk the cream and buttermilk together. Cover and set in a warm place (a gas oven with just the heat from the pilot light is fine) for 8 hours. Crema may be kept in the refrigerator as long as a week.

TARTS AND PIES

GUAVA CHEESE TART

Serves 8

6 ounces (¾ cup) cream cheese, at room temperature

1 cup grated *panela* or dry-curd farmer cheese

2 (½-pound) pieces puff pastry, each cut into a 12-inch circle

1 egg, lightly beaten

⅔ cup guava paste or other fruit jam or puree mixed with ¼ cup freshly squeezed lime juice

1 tablespoon heavy cream

TART, SWEET GUAVA AND SOOTHING CHEESE IN FLAKY PASTRY IS A TRADITIONAL MEXICAN DESSERT COMBINATION, BUT OUR MORE SOPHISTICATED VERSION ALSO MAKES A WONDERFUL MORNING PASTRY FOR BRUNCH. APRICOT OR RHUBARB WOULD BE GOOD SUBSTITUTES IF GUAVA IS UNAVAILABLE.

Place the cream cheese and *panela* or farmer cheese in a bowl and mix well with a spoon.

Line a baking sheet with parchment paper. Place 1 of the puff pastry circles on the baking sheet. Brush a 1-inch rim around the outside edge with some of the beaten egg. Pat the cheese mixture into an 8-inch circle in the center and spread the guava paste or jam evenly over the top.

Fold the remaining piece of puff pastry in half and place over the first piece. Unfold the pastry to enclose the filling, being careful not to trap air beneath. Gently press the top and bottom edges together and refrigerate about 25 minutes, or until the dough is thoroughly chilled.

Remove from the refrigerator. Working about 1½ inches from the outside, firmly press the edges of pastry together with the tines of a fork to seal. Then trim the excess dough, leaving an even 1-

inch border of crust surrounding the filling. With a sharp paring knife, cut out and discard a ¾-inch circle of dough from the center, and press out any trapped air. Then, making shallow cuts, trace 6 to 8 circular lines in a spiral pattern from the center hole to the inside edge of the sealed crust. (If the dough gets too warm to work with, just return to the refrigerator for 30 minutes or so to harden.)

Mix the heavy cream with the remaining beaten egg and brush over the top of the tart. Cover with plastic wrap and chill at least 2 hours or overnight.

To bake, preheat the oven to 450°F.

Transfer the tart from refrigerator to the oven and bake 15 minutes, or until puffed and golden brown on top. Reduce the oven temperature to 350°F. Bake until the jelly is bubbling and the bottom crust, when lifted with a spatula, is browned, 30 to 40 minutes. Set aside to cool on a rack 10 to 15 minutes. Serve warm.

FRIED APPLE TART

Serves 8

1 (8-ounce) sheet frozen puff pastry dough, thawed

1/2 cup water

1 cup sugar

6 large Granny Smith apples, peeled, cored and cut into 10 wedges each

4 tablespoons unsalted butter, cut into pieces

HERE IS A SIMPLIFIED, NOT SO MEXICAN, BUT FOOLPROOF VERSION OF THE CLASSIC FRENCH UPSIDE DOWN APPLE TART, TARTE TATIN. IT IS SIMPLY WONDERFUL SERVED WITH SCOOPS OF HOMEMADE VANILLA ICE CREAM.

Preheat the oven to 425°F.

On a floured surface, thaw the pastry, roll out to a 1/4-inch thickness and cut out a 10-inch circle. Crimp the edges to form a rim and pierce all over with the tines of a fork. Place on a cookie sheet and refrigerate 15 minutes to 1 hour.

Bake the pastry crust until golden brown, 10 to 15 minutes. Set aside.

Combine the water and sugar in a large skillet over high heat. Cook, swirling the pan frequently, until the mixture is deep brown with the fragrance of caramel, about 10 minutes. Add the apples and butter. Toss with a wooden spoon to evenly coat and continue cooking over high heat until the caramel begins to thicken and the apples are well coated and puffy, 10 to 13 minutes.

Strain the apples, reserving their caramelized juices. Set the apples aside to cool 15 minutes.

When cool enough to handle, arrange the apples in overlapping concentric circles over the puff pastry crust. You may need to press the apples slightly to flatten and cover any spaces. Pour on the caramelized juices and serve immediately.

LIME COCONUT PIE

Serves 8

CRUST AND TOPPING

¾ cups sugar cookie or graham cracker crumbs

2¼ cups sweetened shredded coconut

1 tablespoon unsalted butter, melted

LIME CURD

4 tablespoons unsalted butter

¾ cup freshly squeezed lime juice

2 tablespoons cornmeal

pinch of salt

1¼ cups sugar

4 large eggs, separated

2 large egg yolks

¼ teaspoon cream of tartar

finely grated zest of 1 lime

WITH ITS MOUNTAIN OF TOASTED SHREDDED COCONUT ON A GENEROUS BED OF COOL LIME CUSTARD, THIS IS A MOST IMPRESSIVE SUMMERTIME DESSERT. BEGIN A DAY AHEAD SO THE LIME CURD HAS A CHANCE TO PROPERLY SET.

Combine the crust and topping ingredients. Press one half of the mixture into the bottom and sides of an ungreased 10-inch glass or ceramic pie plate, building up the sides to the top of the plate to form an edge. Reserve remaining mixture for the topping.

To make the lime curd, combine the butter, lime juice, cornmeal, salt and ¾ cup of the sugar in a large bowl over a pan of simmering water with the bottom not touching the water, and slowly cook, scraping the sides of the bowl and whisking occasionally, 15 minutes. Add the yolks, all at once, and cook, whisking occasionally, another 15 minutes, or until thickened. Cover with plastic and refrigerate. Stir the curd every 10 minutes or so to cool evenly.

Preheat the oven to 275°F.

In a clean bowl, beat the egg whites with the cream of tartar and the remaining ½ cup sugar until stiff and glossy. Gently fold half of the beaten whites into the cool lime curd to lighten. Then fold in the remaining whites and the lime zest. (This should be very gentle; it is okay for a few streaks of white to be showing.)

Pour the filling into the pie shell and sprinkle on reserved topping evenly to cover. Gently press the sides in so the top ½ inch of crust remains bare. Bake 45 minutes, or until the pie has risen and coconut is golden brown. The filling should be slightly cracked and firm when pressed in the center. Cool completely, cover with plastic and refrigerate 6 hours to chill thoroughly. Serve cold.

CHOCOLATE CREAM PIE

Serves 8 to 10

1 cup slivered almonds

3 large egg whites

¾ cup granulated sugar

½ teaspoon cream of tartar

7 ounces semisweet chocolate, chopped

1 ounce unsweetened chocolate, chopped

2¼ cups heavy cream, cold

⅓ cup confectioners' sugar

¾ teaspoon ground cinnamon

¾ teaspoon vanilla extract

4 to 6 ounces bittersweet chocolate, grated or shaved into curls, for garnish (optional)

WE LIKE TO MIX DIFFERENT CHOCOLATES FOR A MORE COMPLEX FLAVOR IN OUR CHOCOLATE DESSERTS. IN THIS RICH PIE TWO CHOCOLATES ARE MIXED WITH CINNAMON AND ALMONDS, TYPICAL MEXICAN FLAVORINGS, AND THEN SERVED IN A CRISP MERINGUE SHELL. WHENEVER RECIPES CALL FOR YOLKS ONLY, BE SURE TO SAVE THE WHITES IN THE FREEZER, SINCE THEY DEFROST QUICKLY AND WHIP UP EVEN BETTER AS THEY AGE.

Preheat the oven to 350°F.

Spread the almonds on a cookie sheet and toast in the oven until golden, about 15 minutes. Set aside to cool.

Turn the oven down to 275°F. Butter the bottom and sides (not the lip) of a 9-inch glass pie plate.

Place the egg whites in the bowl of an electric mixer and set over a pan of hot tap water until slightly warmed. Then whisk the warm egg whites until soft peaks form. Whisk in the cream of tartar and then add the granulated sugar in a slow, steady stream, whisking continuously. Continue whisking until stiff and glossy, 15 to 20 minutes longer.

Make a pie shell with the meringue by smoothing it over the bottom and sides of the buttered pie plate. Bake until slightly crisp and dry, 15 minutes. Cool on a rack.

Combine the two chocolates in a bowl over simmering water, and stir occasionally until melted. Let cool to room temperature.

Combine the heavy cream, confectioners' sugar, cinnamon and vanilla in a mixing bowl. Beat at medium speed until *very* soft peaks form, 2 to 3 minutes. Stir one-third of the cream into the melted chocolates to lighten. Then add that mixture to the whipped cream and fold in until completely incorporated.

Scatter half of the toasted almonds over the cooked meringue shell. Top with the chocolate cream filling, smoothing the top. Decorate the top with the remaining toasted almonds and grated chocolate or chocolate curls, if desired. Cover and refrigerate at least 1 hour before serving.

CARAMEL APPLE PIE

Serves 10

Pie Dough, recipe follows

7 large Granny Smith or Pippin apples, peeled and cored

1 cup sugar

3 tablespoons quick-cooking tapioca

1 teaspoon ground cinnamon

½ teaspoon salt

juice of ½ lemon

1 tablespoon heavy cream

1 large egg

Caramel Topping, recipe follows

THIS OVERSTUFFED PIE TAKES A CLASSIC COMBINATION OF CHILDHOOD—APPLES AND CARAMEL—AND TRANSFORMS IT INTO AN IMPRESSIVE ADULT DESSERT. AT THE RESTAURANT WE SERVE IT HOT WITH A SCOOP OF CINNAMON PECAN ICE CREAM (PAGE 242), BUT VANILLA ICE CREAM WILL DO JUST FINE.

Butter and flour a 9-inch glass pie plate.

On a lightly floured surface, roll out half the dough to a 12-inch round about ⅛ inch thick. Line the pie plate, being sure to press the dough into the bottom and up the sides without stretching. Chill for 30 minutes.

Roughly chop the apples into small pieces, about the size of lima beans. (The apples should measure about 9 cups chopped.) Combine with the sugar, tapioca, cinnamon, salt and lemon juice in a large bowl. Set aside until the juices begin to run, 10 to 15 minutes.

Meanwhile, beat together the cream and egg to make a glaze and brush over the edges of the bottom crust.

Mound the apple filling in the pie shell. It will be quite full.

Roll out the remaining dough to a large round about ⅛ inch thick. Place over the filling and seal the edges together by gently pressing together. Trim any excess dough with scissors and flute the edges. Brush the top with the remaining egg glaze.

Using a paring knife, cut out and remove a circle the size of a quarter from the center of the top crust. Cut 5 or 6 slits in a spoke pattern, beginning ½ inch from the center hole and ending ½ inch from the outside edge. Chill for 30 minutes before baking.

Preheat the oven to 425° F.

Place the pie plate on a cookie sheet and bake 10 to 15 minutes, or until the top is golden brown. Reduce the heat to 300°F and continue baking until the juices visible in the center are thick and bubbly, about 1 hour. (If the edges are browning too quickly, cover with aluminum foil.)

Meanwhile, make the Caramel Topping.

Spoon the hot caramel over the top of the pie to coat and return to the oven. Bake 5 minutes longer, or until the caramel sets. Cool on a rack before serving.

PIE DOUGH

Makes two 9- or 10-inch pie crusts

2 cups all-purpose flour

1/2 cup lard

2 1/2 tablespoons unsalted butter

1/2 teaspoon salt

about 1/2 cup iced water

CARAMEL TOPPING

1/2 cup packed brown sugar

4 tablespoons unsalted butter

2 tablespoons heavy cream

1/2 cup pecan halves

In a large bowl, combine the flour with the lard, butter and salt. Mix lightly with your fingertips until the dough forms grape-sized pieces. You should still be able to see chunks of fat.

Stir in the iced water. Lightly knead, handling the dough as little as possible, until the dough forms a ball. Add a little more iced water if necessary.

Transfer to a plastic bag and shape into a log. Seal the bag, pressing out any air, and chill 1 hour or as long as 3 days. The pie dough can be frozen for as long as a week.

Combine the brown sugar, butter and cream in a small saucepan. Bring to a boil and cook for 2 minutes. Remove from the heat and stir in the pecan halves.

INDEX